Everything You Need To Know About Making Serious Money Trading The Financial Markets

Simon W

This book is dedicated to my son, James Harper-Watkins

Two

12⁰⁰

4/14

ADVFN BOOKS

CONTENTS

Psychology Of Trading

The Competition

As in life in general, in trading as well it is important to know who you are up against, because trading is a zero sum game as far as each individual is concerned: one either wins or one loses, over time, and, ultimately, it will always be at someone else's expense.

The market consists broadly of two types of investors: **institutional ones (huge) and retail ones (small)**. The general parameters of this investment universe are simple enough: in 2009, it was measured that retail traders (RT) on average are responsible for about USD110bn in currency flows across options, swaps, futures and spot forex in total per day; the figure for institutional investors (II), though, was around USD3.2trn. Nowadays, the proportions are basically the same, according to the latest (2013) Triennial FX Survey from the Bank for International Settlements in Basel, although the retail sector's share has increased slightly as the development of retail trading platforms has picked up pace, and the total amount of FX trading on average per day was USD5.3trn at the time of the Survey.

One key factor that all retail traders should bear in mind, and a principal reason for reading this book, is that around 90% of all retail traders lose all of their trading money within about 90 days. The 90% that lose it are those who have little grasp of the realities, technicalities, psychology and nature of all major traded financial markets around the globe; a solid knowledge of these is an absolute, unequivocal prerequisite to being one of the 1% of retail traders who make very serious, life-changing amounts money by trading the global financial markets. The other 9% can look forward to making significant money from such trading, even on a part-time basis, IF they know the cornerstones that have defined trading activity ever since it began.

More specifically, to begin with then, the retail trader would be well advised to learn how to read the psychology behind these institutional investment flows and ride along with them, at least in the beginning. However, within this idea, the retail investor also needs to recognise that not all institutional investors (II) are the same. Again, in broad terms, one can regard IIs as being either **'real money funds' (RMFs)**, which encompasses those funds looking to generate steady, sustainable returns over time for their investors (such as pension funds, insurance companies and so on) and **hedge funds (HFs)**, which, despite the conservative nature implied in the nomenclature, are usually at the end of sharper, shorter, more violent moves in the market.

Looking at the charts below, I have delineated the nature of the types of move that both of these sorts of funds might typically be behind.

Before we get cracking, though, for those who have traded non-FX assets in the past or have not traded at all, here's a reprise of the basic conventions of FX trading:

- In any single FX transaction there is a base currency (quoted on the left) and a counter-currency (quoted on the right). For example: US dollar (base currency) vs Japanese yen (counter-currency);

- All currencies have a three letter dealing code, the first two letters of which are generally an abbreviation of the country of origin (in the above case US or JP) and the final one is the first letter of the actual currency (in the above case D or Y).
  Therefore, the above currency pair would have the designation of USDJPY;

- The standard market practice is to take the currency that has historically been the dominant one as the base (USD is common, but the notable exceptions to this are GBP, which is nearly always the base, and EUR, which is now generally taken as the base against any other currency against which it is quoted);

- The price quoted will be the number of the counter-currency units to a single unit of the base currency. For example, in the above case, USDJPY87.65 means that one has to sell 87.65 yen for each dollar purchased;

- In the above example, the pair is quoted to just two decimal places, which is normal for the yen in particular, but usually FX quotes are to four decimal places. For example, EURUSD would be quoted as EURUSD1.2570/75; and

- In this quote, dealers give a bid price (the price at which they will buy euros and sell USD) on the left and an offer price (the price at which they will sell euros and buy USD) on the right. Rather than saying EURUSD1.2570 1.2575, the offer price is shortened to just the last two decimal places; so, "70, 75."

So, here we go on dealing proper.

Real Money Funds

EURUSD (3 Years, Daily)

FX:EURUSD (Euro (B) VS United States Dollar Spot (Eur/USD))
Open: 1.3677 High: 1.3685 Low: 1.3634 Cur: 1.3646 (-00.00308/-00.23%)

(c) www.advfn.com

[Chart Key:
A = RMFs sell EURUSD at 1.4500
B = RMFs take part-profit around 1.3500, so 7% return banked
C = RMFs buy back remainder @ 1.2200, so 16% profit all in]

Each real money fund would have formed **their own particular rationale** underpinning why they should short the EUR but a common – and entirely reasonable – one when the first wave of major all-out selling of the euro began in its own right (around 2009) stems from the general thesis that the inhabitants of Europe do not broadly think of themselves in notional ideological terms as being 'European' or even Northern European or Southern European, but rather in practical nationalistic terms as being German, French, Italian and so on.

In this profoundly basic context, a paradox lies at the heart of the European Union: it is designed to create a pan-European identity amongst a diverse range of peoples who fundamentally do not, and have never, seen themselves as anything other than citizens of nation states, each with their own individual language, culture, history and traditions.

This is why the once much-vaunted pan-European language of Esperanto still has but a handful of speakers and is not the language of business in the region. It is also why there is neither a common EU foreign policy, nor one of defence, nor indeed – and this is at the epicentre of the current crisis, of course – shared banking or budgetary policies.

Further still, this fundamental nationalism across EU states means that there is an endemic reluctance on the part of the more industrialised and wealthier countries of Northern Europe to assist the softer economies of Southern Europe, particularly when they are regarded as profligate. This was evident in all recent German regional elections and was particularly noticeable in the first elections in North Rhine-Westphalia after problems in the eurozone became more obvious, in which German Chancellor Angela Merkel's CDU lost control, largely, according to opinion polls at the time, on voters' anger over the Greece bailout package.

And so the argument would run, a fundamental rationale for selling EURUSD was born.

As it transpired, such a strategy bore excellent results until the European Central Bank – in common with other major central banks around the globe – had their policy remit widened to go beyond that of dealing solely with pricing, with a **notional return on capital of 16% in just five months** on shorts taken out at EURUSD1.4500 and liquidated around the EURUSD1.2200 level. But the key point here is **that many real money funds entered into these trades, especially in the equities arena, as bottom-drawer trades**, for which they had a fundamental broad-based rationale that allowed them to feel secure in their trade and happy to hang on to them largely for as long as they felt that the fundamentals still justified them. In my opinion, all of these negative factors surrounding the fundamental disjuncture lying at the heart of the eurozone project, and a reason for selling the euro on any significant rallies, still remain in place.

Along the way, of course, nice little bonuses came along to ensure that these funds could hold these short positions longer than perhaps they had at first intended (EURUSD1.3000 was the initial buyback target level for much of this money) – such as the Germans' imposition of a ban on short-selling of various financial products (which smacked of weakness, and the markets can be viewed as an ocean teaming with sharks waiting for the taste of blood in the water, *see below*) and concomitant worsening situations in Spain, Ireland, Italy, Portugal and most latterly even France. Not to mention, the added impetus of hedge funds shorting all the way along the line for a sustained period.

Hedge Funds

EURUSD (3 Years, Daily)

FX:EURUSD (Euro (B) VS United States Dollar Spot (Eur/USD))
Open: 1.3677 High: 1.3685 Low: 1.3634 Cur: 1.3651 (-00.00258/-00.19%)

(c) www.advfn.com

[Chart Key:
A = HFs sell at key technical resistance level
B = HFs sell again at next major technical level
C = HFs buy back shorts aggressively, morphing into going net long
D = HFs sell out all longs]

The above chart shows a number of key facets of hedge fund trading of which the retail trader needs to be aware. To begin with, it is wise to note that the underlying rationale behind the trade may well have been the same as for the RMFs but **hedge funds will add dynamic and aggressive intraday trading tactics to the mix**.

In the above example, for instance, most of the **major moves happen overnight or in other periods in which the market is relatively illiquid**. This is a classic hedge fund strategy. It means that less money can have a disproportionately great effect on the price than in normal liquid conditions. If you have a £10 note in your pocket in the company of millionaires you are nothing special, but if you have £10 on a park bench with hobos then you are the king.

Another tactic frequently employed by hedge funds is to **trend the market in one direction, encouraging others (especially retail traders) to follow that trend and then to rapidly square off that position and simultaneously take the opposite one**.

In this instance, those RT who do not read top-notch market analysis and monitor trading flows will find their short EURUSD positions going quickly against them and then being stopped out (i.e. having to buy back EURUSD). Add in all of these RT stops going through the market in illiquid conditions, and you set the stage for a rapid move back up, which is exactly what the hedge funds wanted in the above example.

A final point of which to be aware is that **hedge funds often choose to launch such ambushes at key technical levels** *(see the Technical Analysis section of this book)* where they know RT investors will be watching closely for directional signs: hence, in the above example, selling at major resistance levels, Fibonacci retracements and so forth. However, it is important to note **that hedge funds often choose to *reverse* these positions at levels which apparently have no technical significance whatsoever,** thus taking everyone by surprise and hijacking market momentum.

Finally, remember that **once hedge funds get it into their collective minds to go after something that they perceive to be weak then there is little any other trader – except the central banks nowadays – can do to alter their path, so hop on board the ride**, if you think the move is genuine.

Quite aside from the EUR, another great case in point was sterling under the John Major government and Norman Lamont's Chancellorship. Hedge funds, along, to be fair, with most others in the market eventually, did not think that GBP was ready to be in the Exchange Rate Mechanism (ERM), with its narrow trading fluctuation bands.

Hedge funds, and George Soros perhaps most notably, decided to go after the currency and proprietary trading desks at banks jumped on the bandwagon. Despite massive buying of sterling by the UK government, which also raised interest rates repeatedly (which should theoretically have supported GBP, as money goes to where it is best rewarded – *see the Risk Management section of this book*), the Major government had no choice but to withdraw from the ERM.

Moreover, as has been evidenced with the EUR, once the market has rinsed all value out of one target (initially, Greece), it will then look for the next weakest in the conceptual chain (e.g. Spain, Portugal and so on).

Therefore, in addition to jumping on the short EUR bandwagon, a good trader would have spotted that Spanish equities' valuations were high and sold those too, and the same with Portugal, for example.

Greed And Fear

No matter how high-minded one might think oneself, the aforementioned two emotions are the prevailing ones in trading, and despite what Gordon Gekko (whose character, by the way, was reputedly based on an amalgam of one-time junk bond king Michael Milken and corporate raider, Ivan Boesky – both of whom went to prison for a while) said, greed is not good and neither is fear.

Greed manifests itself most palpably during bull trends, and the less experience/discipline one has, the more one succumbs to its ill-effects on trading strategy. In a bull trend, by definition, there are, in simple terms, more buyers than sellers: which is fine. The problem for the RT comes when he gets greedy for further profits (provided he is long) and decides to hold his position for that bit longer, just to capitalise on his good fortune. The logical outcome of this is that he will hold on to his position until such a point that the trade starts to reverse and go down. Unfortunately, particularly in FX, this turnaround can happen extremely quickly and all the more so if there is a significant presence of hedge fund money in the market (*see above Hedge Fund chart*).

At this point, the prevailing emotion is still greed, as the trader begins to fret that he has not taken all the profit he could, and waits for his position to go back up again to the point at which he could have sold out and taken profit about five minutes earlier. 'Sod's Law' here is that, of course, it will continue to go down, at which point the RT's prevailing emotion starts to change to fear. Fear that he cannot get out of his position except at lower levels, and greater fear as all his profit is wiped out and his position starts to go into the red.

And that neatly brings us on to the next bit, which, together with Effective Order Placement and solid Technical Analysis, should form the cornerstone to the overall strategy of not getting caught out in the vicissitudes of greed and fear that will ultimately destroy one's trading account, not to mention one's sanity.

The Markets Look For Signs Of Weakness

The markets can be regarded as a vast ocean filled with sharks waiting to sense the blood of the stricken and then moving in for the kill. They are a place in which no one wishes you well unless they know that you are terminally ill. They are not a place, in short, for the faint-hearted.

From the perspective of the RT, they can appear daunting, but there are a number of key elements that one can employ that can serve to turn oneself from a potential loser into a real winner.

Trading Is A Lonely Occupation

I have sat in dealing rooms with more than 500 other traders in them and felt completely isolated when I have a trade going against me; everyone will experience this feeling at some time in their trading careers: it goes with the territory. **Discussing it with others is a bad idea**, because: first, they will not care at all and will probably spend their time winding you up about your misfortune instead, making matters worse; and second, everyone else will know your trading position, which is never advisable, and it inevitably will be used against you somewhere along the line (as I told you, trading is, ultimately, a zero-sum game).

Self-Flagellation And Knee-Jerk Trading

Loneliness during trading can have two major negative effects on one's profitability, if it is not recognised and managed effectively: first, it can make one **question the validity of the ideas underpinning one's trade**; and second, it can **lead to 'knee-jerk' trading**, in which the RT nervously exits a perfectly sound position, changes direction then trades out of that and so on.

In the event of the first scenario, one should go back through the fundamental rationale for the trade, re-examine the technical levels (Support and Resistance levels, Fibonacci retracements, Moving Averages, RSI and so on – *see the Technical Analysis section*), gauge prevailing market sentiment and, if all of these are still sound, then hold the position or try hedging all or part of it – *see the Risk Management section*. In the second scenario, again do what one did in the first.

Gap Trading

In a truly efficient market (one in which every participant knows the true price and what everyone else's position is, which is open all the time and so on), the ebb and flow of pricing would be seamless, up or down.

However, this is not always true in practice, and in some conditions markets tend to 'gap' – that is, they jump from one price to a much higher/lower level without going gradually through a graduated pricing pattern beforehand.

Dynamic Of Gap Times (applies to a lesser degree to FX, which is 24/6 but slighter volumes will usually be noticed in these gap periods): Japanese and Asia and Australasia session 00:30-07:30 GMT/Gap Time 07:30-08:00 GMT/London and European Session 08:00-13:00 GMT/Gap Time 13:00-3:30 GMT/US Session 13:30-20:30 GMT/Gap Time 20:30-00:30 GMT.

It is apposite to note that the most liquid market is when the London and New York markets are open at the same time, and the least liquid is when only Asia and Australasia are in the game.

This gap phenomenon usually appears in markets that are not 24/6 (as the FX market is). For example, if one is trading the FTSE100 then it is clear that there is a timing gap between when the FTSE closes on Friday and when it reopens on Monday morning at 8am GMT, as illustrated in the chart below.

FTSE100 (3 Months, Daily)

[Chart Key:

Gap A = RSI shows no real buying momentum — the smart money is looking to sell on rallies, whilst the hysterical money is chasing the tail of the last move up

Gap B = Same pattern as in the previous example — hysterical money is still convinced it is going up but smart money is not — hence the small candlesticks

Gap C = With a new week, the smart money has made its profits on shorts and is now going long — with more commitment shown by longer candlesticks]

Above we can see from the RSI trends that there is only one real move up based on 'smart money': that punctuated by Gap C. In the latter event, the 'hysterical money' is chasing the tail of the move or incorrectly anticipating the level at which the smart money may take profits on shorts.

In smart money moves, the candlesticks themselves tend to be bigger than in hysterical money moves, which are shorter and often punctuated by small reversals (i.e. lack of confidence in one's fundamental positioning).

With Gap Trading, though, even as an RT one can make good money by correctly identifying the overall trend, both from the price action on the foremost graph and from the underlying momentum underpinning the trade trend (from RSI, Price Oscillator, MACD and so on).

In FX, as well, Gap Trading occurs, and oftentimes this occurs after major economic figures (or a change in credit rating for a country, a natural disaster or unexpected political change).

AUDUSD (3 Months, Daily)

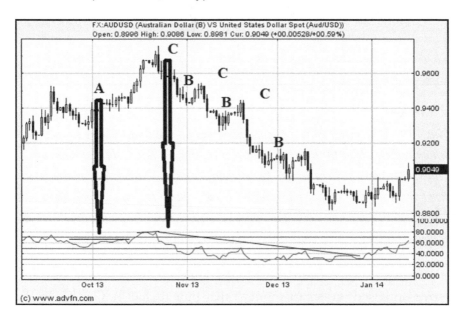

[Chart Key:
A = Hysterical money is on the end of a move up, but RSI shows no real upwards price momentum
B = Hysterical money still looking for it to go higher, but RSI bias is for weakness

C = Hysterical money uses this gap to buy into existing longs, allowing smart money to go short at better levels]

However, by not looking at the RSI (or any other momentum indicator) and misusing the gap to trade on a signal that does not exist and has not been confirmed, combined with no knowledge of the longer-term trend being followed by the smart money, the hysterical money is about to be screwed.

In determining which way the smart money – or more particularly, the weight of smart money – is going, a good tool is to regard charts as combinations of *'impulse' moves* and *'corrective' moves.*

In this context, in short, an **impulsive move** is one that covers more pips in less time than a corrective one. Additionally, impulsive moves are characterised by longer candlesticks than corrective ones. And finally, impulse moves comprise several of the same coloured candlesticks in a row.

Conversely, a **corrective move** is characterised by a more even distribution of bull and bear candlesticks and by the emergence of more wicks/tails on the candle's extreme points. Additionally, a corrective move will be made up of a more balanced mixture of winning candlesticks against losing ones (ie the number of pips made against the number of pips lost).

AUDUSD (1 Year, Daily)

As in the chart above, it is clear that the move down on AUDUSD had heavy money behind it, eventually both a mixture of a broad-based corrective moves and of sudden impulsive moves on the back of those, and it was not going to turn on short-term RT trading against it. In this respect it is rather similar to trying to stop a charging bull elephant with a pea-shooter.

In summary, the overall downmove covered by the corrective pattern box above was 848 pips but, as can be seen, three of these one-way (impulse pattern) moves accounted for 646 pips of that. The impulsive moves were marked, as mentioned, by one-way trading (back to back black candles in this diagram, denoting selling) that are much longer than the bid candles showing fast, determined price action.

A generally sound policy to find a good entry position for the day ahead is to **watch the market for around half an hour before the**

start of the session (in the case of FX in London, you should be watching it from around 6am GMT at the latest).

If the **price drops below the most recent significant low but does not hold there for more than a few minutes (tops) then a rule of thumb is that players are trying to find better levels to go long/add to long positions** by temporarily selling the currency pair down in slim market volume conditions.

Therefore, **and taking into account all the preparation of support and resistance levels, general economic and political overview, RSI analysis, MACD** etc, if a long still makes sense then go long when the price starts to dip down to the level at which you think the other players were trying to get long. And, of course, the reverse is true.

In this context, the breaking of recent lows and highs at the beginning/end of a session is often a signal of opposite orders being filled at a better price. This will tell you where the smart money is positioning itself (together with the other factors discussed above).

In the above example, of course, make use of effective order management, as previously discussed.

Account Size And Setting Targets

In order to have any peace of mind as a trader, one requires an account with sufficient capital for one's trading ambitions. Or, conversely, one needs to have trading ambitions that are cut according to one's capital. One cannot have an imbalance here.

It is true that, **with a £500 initial stake in an account, one can, in theory – and no doubt it has been done in practice – become a millionaire within five years (*see chart below*)**, if one doubles one's money every six months, as the table below illustrates:

Capital Accumulation Over Six Years From An Initial £500 Investment	
Months	Capital
0	500
6	1000
12	2000
18	4000
24	8000
30	16000
36	32000
42	64000
48	128000
54	256000
60	512000
66	1024000
72	2048000

This, though, requires a high degree of self-discipline *(see below)*, excellent order management *(see below)*, excellent market knowledge and contacts *(see below)* and highly developed skills of technical analysis *(see the Technical Analysis section)*.

In terms of self-discipline first, **cut your profit target according to your account balance**. You should, at minimum, set a risk/reward ratio of 4:1 in the first few years of trading on your own account – that is, for every £1 you might stand to lose you could make £4.

Second, if you are trying to double your money over the 0-6 month period then you must make £500. Split down £500 into weeks, for a weekly profit target: thus, the weekly profit target for you is £500/26 = £19 per week.

Concomitant with this, you need to **work out how much is the maximum that you can place on any one trade**. As I have mentioned, **professional bank/fund management traders will typically risk anywhere between 1%-5% of their capital on any single trade. I suggest that, to begin with, you risk no more**

than 1% of your capital on any one trade. Therefore, on any single trade, you can risk no more than £5 in total.

This is clearly not much, if you are doing £1 per pip, which is why I become somewhat irritated by companies who tell you that all you need to start trading is £500. **It is true that some trading platforms allow you to trade a minimum lot size of 50p per point, which is one way of circumventing extremely limited capital in an account.** Another is to try to trade £1 per pip, but this allows you absolutely no real room for error, as the spread alone (the difference between a trading platform's bid and offer prices for the base currency in a currency pair) is often at least 3 pips. On this basis, you cannot afford for the pair to move more than 2 more pips, which clearly is insane.

Therefore, **I would suggest that a minimum sensible amount to have in a trading account to begin with is between £5000-£10,000.** This allows you flexibility in hedging ongoing positions that are not performing well in the very short-term but that one believes (based on empirical evidence) will come good in the slightly longer term. And, of course, the doubling process outlined in the earlier chart is still the same.

In order to make £10,000, one must make a weekly profit of £385 per week over six months. 1% of £10,000 is obviously £100, which means that is one's stop-loss. At £1 per pip that is a 100 pip movement against you that is acceptable, which is relatively reasonable in a market of average volatility. Indeed, it may be that, under these conditions, one might consider putting £2 per pip on the trade, whilst simultaneously cutting one's stop-loss to 50 pips from the point of trade entry. As such, it is fairly straightforward and realistic to make the required sum in the target period and even more quickly if using weightings across different asset classes, given proper risk management.

USDCAD (6 Months, Daily)

[Chart Key:

A = Buys USD and against CAD

B = Becomes jittery with some money in the bank, and takes a small profit on the whole lot

C = Remembers the sound reasons that he went long USDCAD in the first place, and is bored anyhow, so goes long again

D = Gets worried about his losing position, so closes it out for a small loss and, trying to ride the reverse idea, goes short in tandem with the very short-term price action

E = Gets worried about his short, so tries to average it out by going shorter higher up

F = It looks like it's going his way again, so adds to short

G = Bereft, desolate and with a lot less money; if only he had stuck to his first idea, put the trade on with a tight stop loss order and gone golfing instead]

In the above example, for instance, a lot of stress could have been avoided and money could have been made by simply putting an order on to buy USD at 1.0290, with a stop loss order, i.e. selling USDCAD at 1.0190 (at £1 per pip, the maximum loss would be £100, within the daily limit if there is £10,000 in the trading account) and riding the upside based on technical. He could also have just left a take profit order again based on key resistance points; no stress, no hassle, a vastly improved golf game over time.

Contrarian Trading

Given what we know about the weight of money that real money funds and hedge funds bash around in the market, it might seem that trading contrary to the present trend direction is an insane choice of dealing style. And it is, if one does not know what one is doing, but that applies to all forms of trading in the first place.

The key to this type of trading, though, is to **look at the markets in terms of the sentiment of those participating in it**, to gauge when is the right time to buy and when the right time to sell, whilst using all of the factors that have been discussed in this book.

COT

Sentiment underpinning a trend can be gleaned, among other things, from the aptly named '**Commitment of Traders Report**' (COT), which is available for free on the Commodities Futures Trading Commission (**CFTC**) website, to be precise http://www.cmegroup.com/trading/fx/cftc-tff/main.html.
Although this is data that applies specifically to the futures market, it is equally applicable to sentiment in the spot FX market and other asset markets (and it is updated every Friday).

COT Charts Are A Key To Gauging Trading Sentiment

HFs

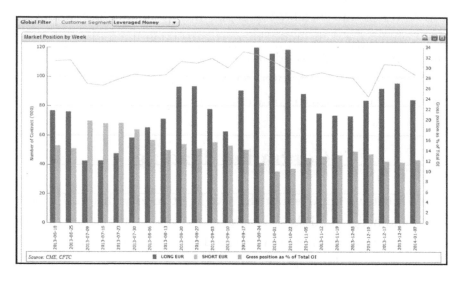

RMFs

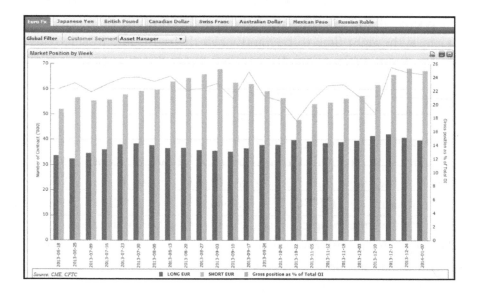

Basically, the usefulness of the COT is that it **shows the net long/short positions for every available futures contract for commercial (hedgers) and non-commercial traders (speculators**, including currency traders, equities traders and commodities traders), among others. As some of these futures contracts are simply hedges against real tangible positions (construction companies selling copper futures in order to hedge their need for copper in house building, for example) these contracts give excellent indications of powerful trends at one extreme end of the market.

As a rule of thumb, speculators tend to buy the market when it is still rising whereas hedgers tend to sell into any rises (and vice-versa for a falling market, of course). In a rising market, therefore, when hedgers' bets are increasing substantially and/or those of speculators are diminishing in tandem then the top of the market cannot be that far away.

This is why it is important to use other technical indicators to assess exactly at what level one is going to exit a long position or enter a new short position.

The VIX

The Volatility Index (VIX) measures the **implied (not historic) volatility of the options bought and sold on the S&P500 US stock index** and therefore is useful for looking at currency pairs that correlate well to movements in this index. The VIX can be found on the Chicago Board Options Exchange (CBOE) website, under the symbol 'VIX' (specifically:
http://www.cboe.com/micro/VIX/vixintro.aspx).

CBOE Volatility Index (VIX) Is A Good Indicator Of Some Trend Reversals

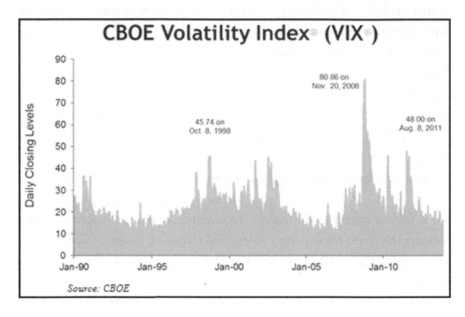

In broad terms, of course, volatility is measure of deviation of market prices from the average mean price over a specified period of time (achieved by looking at Moving Averages, as described above).

Given that options are usually associated with hedging positions against adverse price movements (normally, therefore, they can be seen as protection against a reversal in the present trend) then **one can assume that generally the greater the VIX, the greater the fear amongst followers of trend only that a reversal is on the cards**.

At this point, a position can be liquidated (or opposite position put into place) or the RT can examine other trading options.

Effective Order Management

This brings us to **effective order management** again. The best traders that I have met (as clients or competitors) used orders to their advantage, not just in establishing entry and exit points but in managing their own psychologies. The best I ever met would arrive early in the morning (by the way, to be successful, one needs to **be at one's desk for 6am GMT** at the latest, having read everything that there is to read on the markets and spoken to every contact one can think of about their views), would put on his carefully worked out trades, three or four normally that they had been following ultra-closely for a long time, concomitantly put his stop-loss orders on and then leave again, either to go sailing or play golf. He retired at 25 with a personal worth of around £200mn.

Such a strategy avoids 'knee-jerk' trading, particularly for the RT, who is usually on his/her own throughout the day, with nothing much to do except read and talk more about the markets, look at the trading screens or gaze at the walls. In this scenario, as I mentioned, the **temptation is to reverse perfectly reasonable trades** many times, which will inevitably lead to sustained losses. Another **temptation is to keep trading** to occupy one's time, even if one is up on the day, and this is equally fatal for one's capital.

Obtain The Direct Telephone Number Of Your Platform's Dealing Desk

A number of trading platforms, during times of heightened market risk (when major figures are coming out/have just come out or major unexpected events occur, freeze, and you cannot get a price for love nor money on the screen.

This will drive you nuts and potentially lose you money.

Talking to the back office staff under these circumstances will not help in either of the above mentioned considerations.

Therefore, from before you even start trading a penny, obtain the direct telephone number of the dealing desk itself for whatever asset you are intending to trade and stick it on your screen somewhere.

In the event of a freeze, call the dealers up immediately, tell them you cannot get a price, give them your account number and ask them for a level; then you can deal/pass as you see fit.

A couple of things to note with this process:

1. Dealers will be happy enough to help you, as you are a client.

2. Do not tell them your life story/feelings about your trading/how your pet goldfish is – dealers are extremely busy; be quick, professional and very to the point.

Developing A Rigorous And Sound Personal Trading Methodology

As has been touched on in the above sections, it is essential that one develops one's own personal trading methodology that one feels comfortable with and that one implements it in a rigorous and self-disciplined fashion.

These will vary from person to person, but my own personal methodology, which I used for 10 years as a head of sales and trading for major global banks and for another ten years in personal trading encompasses the following '**Perfect Seven**' items for any trade:

1. Know where the **correct support and resistance levels** are located over different trading periods (1 hour, 1 day, 1 month, 1 year are a good start).

2. Pick out the **overall longer-term trend** to follow, as dictating your overall strategy, whilst also making short-term profits by jobbing in and out of the market (based on shorter-term signals, such as MACD and RSI).

3. Look carefully at the **Fibonacci elements** in a trade, using intra-trend Fibonacci levels well.

4. Watch out for **multiple confirmation areas** (for example, where support and resistance levels are also Fibonacci levels, important MAs and crossovers and so forth).

5. **Talk to a select group of other traders** (maximum, I suggest, is three and preferably still in a major bank/fund management dealing room) to get an idea of where the major orders have been placed the big institutions.

6. Know everything you can about the **fundamental economic and political situations** in countries the currencies of which you will be trading and those outside (in trading, everything is connected).

7. Monitor **developing trends in all the major asset classes**, in order to anticipate coming trends in the particular markets in which you are focused.

With this backdrop in place, manage orders sensibly. Decide where the stop-loss should be (based on one's own risk/reward ratio) and where the take-profit should be (based on one's own risk/reward ratio) then stick to them.

Sticking to whatever methodology one has, provided it is sound, and to one's order levels (and thus risk/reward ratio levels) will mean that one has more free time away from just sitting staring at a screen, that one will make money over time and that one will not go completely bonkers.

Daily Chores

In practical terms, it is a good idea, I find, to also have a tried-and-tested routine before I begin trading for the day (whether or not I still have overnight positions running).

First, I put down on a sheet of paper the **current price of the major currencies** (EURUSD, USDCHF, USDJPY and GBPUSD), plus the AUDUSD, NZD/USD and USDCAD. From these, one can start to glean the pervasive risk sentiment in the market. A rising EUR generally means that investor appetite for risk has moved up the risk curve – that is, they are willing to take more risk – which should be cross-checked with other higher-risk currencies, such as the AUD and NZD, which, if the EUR has strengthened, should probably also have strengthened. The reverse, of course, is true. If there is a divergence in patterns then one has to find out what specific reasons are there for the AUD and NZD to weaken if the EUR is strengthening? Of course, one also has to find out why the EUR is strengthening in the first place as well.

This research would involve me **looking at overnight news and data releases** and examining the charts of each to discern trading trends, long and short term (which I would already have done previously, if I had positions on).

Similarly, in order to discern the pervasive risk sentiment of the market, I would **look at the USD against other standard currencies** (GBP is good in this respect, as it is not part of the EUR-zone), as the USD is generally at the moment lower down the risk curve than the EUR.

Then I would **look at the traditional safe-haven assets:** money will flow broadly into CHF, JPY and gold, although this latter haven has been corrupted recently by central bank interference (many banks produce relative risk charts, showing the current 'safe-haven' assets) when there is a sense of heightened risk in the markets and vice-versa when there is not.

Having gauged market sentiment, I **read everything serious** that I can lay my hands on regarding developments overnight. I say 'serious' because reading a number of self-styled 'authoritative publications' can send one entirely up the wrong path. For reasons of legal liability, I cannot name any of these publications; suffice it to say that they are often to be found on the desks of credit ratings agencies' reception areas, which may explain why they failed to downgrade any major Western banks just prior to their complete collapse in the past few years. The chart below (although there are countless examples to choose from) might further help to illustrate my point.

EURUSD (1 Year, Daily)

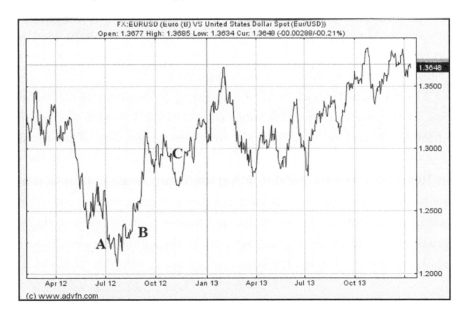

[Chart Key:
A = 'Euro chaos', well respected UK economic and political magazine
B = 'Euro nearing the end of the road', prestigious financial newspaper

C = Euro bears to gather pace, US financial newspaper]

I would then do the **simple technical analysis**, including plotting the day's support and resistance levels (having previously plotted the longer-term ones) and seeing what momentum there is behind different levels (RSI, MA Price Oscillator and so on).

I would then **check the major news and data releases scheduled for the day**, tomorrow and the remainder of the week and month, and make a note of the news/data release, the time (in GMT) that it is expected, what the data/news was on its last release and what the market consensus is for the upcoming release.

Then I would **call two or three contacts in the market** – major dealers at global bank currency desks whom I have known for 20 odd years and whom I trust – and talk to them about their thoughts on the day ahead, making notes as I go.

Then I would have another cup of tea and a cigarette (this is not mandatory, being very bad for my health, so something else is preferred for clients) and mull over everything that I have seen/read/heard in the past hour/couple of hours.

Then I would decide what I am going to do: asset class/classes that I am going to trade, weightings of each, stop-loss and take-profit order levels and possible hedging strategies to get out of positions that turn bad.

Remember as well that **not doing anything is also an option**: if no trade stands out, with at least the correct risk/reward ratio that you have set (this should be at the very least 4:1, all factors remaining equal) then one would be best advised to do something else (read a book unconnected to the markets, go for a walk, feed the goldfish).

Trading Fundamentals

Key Basic Principles

1. Money goes to where it is best rewarded...

Clearly, if one has £100 to invest freely, one is more likely to invest it in a place that provides one with 10% interest per year rather than 0% interest per year.

Exactly the same basic principle applies to FX (or any asset class for that matter) as currencies that are purchased afford the holder an interest rate return (yield) and those which are sold mean that the trader has forfeited the interest accrued on those holdings.

This alludes to the **'Time Value of Money'**, which essentially seeks to put a number on the marginal return that an investor will achieve by forgoing GBP100 (or whatever amount or currency) in his hand right now against investing it in X asset and having the money back later.

In basic terms, then, if 1 year interest rates on deposit accounts at retail banks in the UK were 10% and one invested GBP100 into such an account then in 1 year one would have £110 back in one's hands (GBP100 initial capital + GBP10 accrued interest, of course).

This notion underpins the pricing of all financial instruments. Bond prices, for example, are worked out as follows:

Bond price = 100 − interest rate (simple as that, pretty much), so that, for example, the face value of a bond would be 100 at 0% annual interest, but if the interest rate went up to 10% then, all other things remaining equal, the price of the bond would be 100-10, so 90, one year away from maturity.

As the maturity date approaches that price would get closer to the face value redemption price of the bond, that is, 100. Thus, the 10 points that you gain over the course of the year is compensation for you holding that bond.

Although the principle of 'money goes to where it is best rewarded' underlies all of FX, its most famous example is the out and out '**Carry Trade**', in which traders borrow a currency on which they have to pay virtually no interest and use the proceeds to invest in a currency on which they receive a greater degree of interest. The classic Carry Trades over the past few years have been: borrowing in JPY or CHF (at next to zero, or indeed, zero interest rates) and buying higher-yielding assets, such as AUD or USD, by way of example.

2. ...Having weighed up the concomitant risks...

In the above example, whilst it makes eminent sense to use one's £100 to borrow CHF to buy AUD, one might think again about borrowing in CHF to buy the Zimbabwean dollar (ZWD). This is the risk premium involved in the trade, which is a second key principle in trading FX and a cornerstone of trading fundamentals. Given the choice currently, one would rather invest the money that one had borrowed in CHF into AUD or USD rather than the ZWD, given the former pair's preferable levels of inflation, economic performance and security, banking system safety and so on.

After all, there would be no point in buying ZWD today – even at an exceptionally competitive rate – only to find that one's holdings had halved in value, as inflation had risen another 100% overnight. Conversely, though, if by some chance Zimbabwe's economy underwent a miraculous change with inflation running at 1% per year, GDP growth registering a healthy 6% per year and BIS banking guidelines introduced safeguarding one's assets in the domestic banking system then buying ZWD would look a lot more appealing.

Of course, the converse was true at the height of the recent banking/economic crisis in the West, which resulted in the risk premium for Western currencies going up, with no concomitant compensation in interest rates, meaning that most Western currencies collapsed (except, of course, the ultra-conservative CHF, which, because of its rock-solid foundations, is known as a safe-haven currency).

In these circumstances, therefore, buying the ZWD was more appealing than before, as the risk premium differentiation between the two sets of currencies had narrowed. This notion underpins the idea of the 'risk curve'.

3. ...Which Is Known As The Risk Curve, But...

This encapsulates the idea that the more risk involved in a currency – which broadly acts, along with bonds and equities, as a proxy for the perceived health of the sovereign country of origin – then the more reward (interest rate) is required. Hence, **the worse an economy is perceived to be doing (gauged by the range of economic and fundamental indicators delineated below) the more reward investors will want as compensation to hold that currency**. And by extension, if that interest rate does not increase then that currency will be unpopular and thus weak.

In very simple terms, returning to our £100 cash in the hand investment scenario, we can view a simple risk curve as follows:

- Keep it in cash where it cannot be found or lost = no risk/no reward.

- Keep it in a bank in a 'safe' country (a relative term nowadays, of course, but let us say the UK) = 1% reward/only risk of the bank going bust.

- Keep it in a bank in a less safe country (let us say, Greece) = 10% reward/higher risk of the bank going bust.

- Invest it into the UK stockmarket, via an index tracker = 15% reward on average/higher risk of a market slump, but this is spread over all of the shares in the index.

- Invest in one particular UK share = 20% reward (dividend)/higher risk of something catastrophic happening to that one particular company (for example, BP's oil spill).

- Invest in commodities/non-government bonds/FX = unlimited reward/unlimited risk (if not handled correctly, which is where education, training, strategy, order placing and risk management strategy come in).

4. ...Supply And Demand Dynamics Are Also Vital...

Each of the above serves to define the demand profile for a currency but, as in all simple economics, there is also the **supply element** of the equation to factor in. So, therefore, a currency can also weaken if a country embarks on a 'quantitative easing' policy – that is, printing money (as the US's Fed has done, and the Bank of Japan, and the Bank of England for a while, among the major central banks) – or if the money supply figures start to rise for other reasons (if it is exporting a lot of goods then people are paying out lots of that currency for those goods and will then sell that currency back into their own currency for day to day living).

5. ...As Are Market Perceptions

The financial markets are a very small, insulated world, in which **it is not just what is real that counts and has trading resonance in** currencies (and other asset classes) but what is perceived to be true or might happen. Consequently, it does not actually matter whether, for example, the eurozone is actually going to break up and with it the EUR but whether dealers perceive that it may and to what degree that perception has taken hold *(see the Risk Curve above)*. As such, most fundamental economic figures are not important so much for what they actually represent but rather for what they portend.

Basic Models

Purchasing Power Parity (PPP)

In basic terms, **this means that two currencies will find an equilibrium point at a level where the same product/service costs the same in each country, having taken into account the exchange rate**.

A commonly used example of this is the McDonalds' 'Big Mac', as the usually redoubtable 'Economist' magazine regularly published its 'Big Mac Index' for precisely the reason of discerning correct PPPs.

So, for example, if a Big Mac costs USD2 in the US and GBP1 in Great Britain then the exchange rate should be, according to the PPP measure, GBP1:USD2.

The PPP, then, reflects inflationary data, as if the Consumer Price Index (CPI) inflation measure went up in Great Britain to a degree that it now cost GBP2 for a Big Mac then the exchange rate would be parity between the two currencies – that is, GBP1:USD1.

Clearly the PPP, alongside other of these measures, are of longer-term use in discerning trading patterns but are quite useful from that perspective alone.

Interest Rate Parity (IRP)

This is much more useful to know in the short term, as it occurs within a relatively quick time of interest rates being adjusted in a currency's country of origin.

IRP is quite simply a function of the notion that money goes to where it is best rewarded, as earlier. So if interest rates in Great Britain are at 1% and in the USA at 1% as well, and the price of a Big Mac is £1 in GBP and $2 in USD (so the exchange rate, according to PPP is GBPUSD2 – the number of the counter-currency, USD, to each single unit of the base currency, GBP) and interest rates in Great Britain double to 2% then, all other things remaining equal, it would mean twice as many USD being held for every GBP than before. Therefore, on this basis alone, the exchange rate would be GBPUSD4.

Key Fundamental Economic Indicators

Interest Rates And Inflation

As alluded to above, **interest rates are perhaps the key determinant in FX rates globally**. Remember, **money goes to where it is best rewarded**. All other factors remaining equal, if one country raises its interest rates to above those of another country then the former's currency will become stronger than the latter's as investment capital moves from the latter to the former.

Interest rates, in basic terms, are a key tool for a government in managing its economy. **If an economy is becoming overheated – i.e. inflation is increasing to beyond the point at which a government deems it healthy (a little inflation is a healthy thing, anything from 1% to 5% as a rule of thumb, depending on whether an economy is 'developed', 'emerging' or 'frontier')**

– then interest rates will go up. This means in practical terms that money becomes more expensive, people spend less, demand decreases, manufacturers cannot increase their prices and thus prices stay the same. And, of course, the converse is true.

The last few years in the West are instructive in this context. In the UK, for example, interest rates were low for many years, meaning that people could borrow money (from banks, on credit cards and so on) for very little in terms of interest repayments.

As such, prices increased, the stock market boomed, house prices boomed and people had lots of 'things' (largely things which they did not need, of course). Eventually this resulted in a housing and stock market bubble, which then spent years bursting.

In fact, this low interest rate scenario usually has the effect of increasing inflation – that is, more people are in a position to buy even, for example, a DVD player, and thus the makers of DVD players raise their prices, increase supply or both.

If inflation is not contained in this scenario then there is the danger that it will spiral out of control, meaning that eventually the increasing price of DVD players would reach such a level that people would have to ask for pay rises. **More pay would mean more money in the economy, which would mean more DVD players being sold, which would mean prices going up further, which means more pay rises and so on and so forth: a never-ending upwards spiral, the logical conclusion of which was found in Weimar Germany where a wheelbarrow full of currency was eventually required to buy a loaf of bread**. Or even today in countries such as Zimbabwe, in which the currency has become meaningless pieces of paper. Indeed, using our UK scenario, in the midst of such increasing supply of money, the value of GBP would collapse as a product of supply and demand. In this event, interest rates would have to rise to curtail price increases and the converse is true.

Consequently, **when figures are released showing that inflation in a country looks to be headed upwards, towards levels that a government will not tolerate (a little inflation is necessary to keep an economy expanding), dealers believe that the likelihood of interest rates being increased has been raised and thus the currency is likely to appreciate (money goes to where it is best rewarded) and the currency will be bought**. And, of course, the converse is true.

The chart below shows the effect that an anticipated increase in interest rates had on the NZD in June 2010; incidentally, this rise was due to growing inflationary pressures in the country. Speculation that the New Zealand government would raise rates began around 8 June; the actual rise was on 10 June.

NZDUSD (4 Years, Weekly)

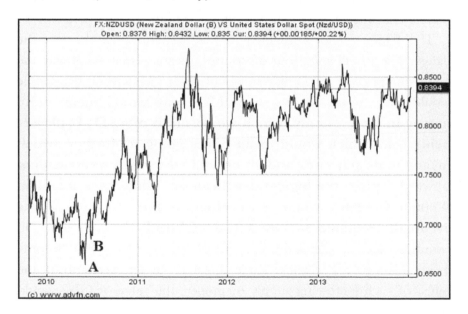

[Chart Key:
A = Market hears rumours that bolster expectations that the central bank will raise interest rates

$B = $ *Interest rates hikes are announced]*

It is apposite to note here that there are **two key inflation figures released by most countries**: the **Consumer Price Index (CPI) and the Producers Price Index (PPI)**. The United Kingdom also introduced the Retail Price Index, which includes items such as housing, which the government tends to play down, as it is often much worse for political purposes than the CPI.

The former can be viewed as prices relating to what people have to spend on a day to day basis to keep their lives ticking over: food, travel, clothing and so on, and this is the more important of the two inflation measures. The latter, in the meantime, deals with expenses that producers of the things people buy incur: machinery, fuel, staplers and so on.

It is apposite to note that **rises/falls in the PPI are often a precursor to the same in the CPI**. This makes sense from the cost-push inflationary aspect as if the prices of raw materials/services used to make goods go up (PPI) then the price of goods/services will tend to go up (CPI).

Trade Flows

As it sounds, these are the **amounts of goods and services that are sold/bought between two countries**, and they have a major effect on currencies, as goods and services bought have to be paid for ultimately in the currency of the country manufacturing these goods or providing these services.

If a country (let us say, the US) buys more goods and services from another country (let us say, Japan) than the other country buys from it then the latter's currency will be prone to rise against the former's. In practical terms, let us return to our DVD scenario (which we will say that only Japan makes and costs USD1) and add a baseball cap scenario (which we will say only the US makes and costs JPY100).

Citizens of the US buy 2 DVDs (JPY200 total), whilst those of Japan buy 1 hat (USD1 total). Japan will then have USD2 in the bank, which it will then sell, buying JPY in order to buy things in Japan. Conversely, the US will then have JPY100, which it will then sell, buying USD in order to buy things in the US. Clearly, then, in this case, twice as many USD are being sold and converted into JPY as the other way around. The logical conclusion of this is that the JPY will become in shorter supply than the USD and that, the laws of supply and demand being as they are, it will rise in value against the USD. In fact, **this is precisely why the JPY has not collapsed during many recent years of complete domestic economic stagnation, as the country was for many years a net exporter (sells more goods and services to other countries than it buys)**.

The apotheosis of this idea is in China (the ultimate net exporter), although here the effect on the currency is dampened because the government manages the CNY very carefully, and instead of allowing it to strengthen markedly (and thus make its goods more expensive relative to those of other exporters) it merely banks the excess foreign currencies in its central bank reserves (which are the largest in the world).

In real trading terms, these trade flows are summed up in a country's **Trade Balance** figure, which shows net exports minus net imports. Over time, an imbalance here will affect a country's currency, for the reason explained above.

In this context, the release of the indices by the US Institute for Supply Management's (ISM) on non-manufacturing businesses (which cover around 90% of the US economy) should be watched closely.

Exactly the same notion applies to a country's **capital flows**, which measures inflows of foreign capital entering a country in order to invest in its markets against outflows. Clearly again, if outflows are greater than inflows then a country's currency is prone to weaken.

GDP

This again is a **huge figure in trading terms, as it measures the rate of expansion/contraction in a country's economy**.

Although it is possible for a country's currency to rise in the absence of economic expansion (Japan, for example), more commonly a currency will go down over time if it is either stagnant or contracting. Aside from anything else, an economy that is not growing will not produce sufficient goods and services to maintain its trade and capital flows and thus, for the reasons outlined above, is prone to decline.

The **real GDP figure is the one to look out for**, as it makes comparisons between different time periods easier, as it takes into account differing levels of inflation.

Additionally important to note is that **the real GDP figure will usually be lower than the CPI** figure, as the former also takes into account the extra portion of investment goods, which are not in the CPI and which tend to have lower inflationary levels than anything contained in the CPI.

Employment

Closely related to GDP and thus once more **a huge figure in trading terms**, employment/unemployment is a sign of economic buoyancy/stagnation which finds its ultimate resolution and clarification in the GDP number, as above, and also in inflation (and thus in interest rates).

High unemployment will result in a lower level of goods and services offered, which, in turn, will affect a country's trade and capital flows and drive a currency down, all other factors

remaining equal. Low unemployment will result in a burgeoning GDP, more positive trade balances and a currency moving up over time. With low employment, though, there is also the spectre of rising inflation, as employed people have more money to spend than unemployed ones, and thus prices tend to rise in such an environment.

However, as mentioned earlier, **inflation only becomes a concern to the market if a government appears to be avoiding measures to tackle it** (Zimbabwe, among others), whereas those governments that increase interest rates will likely benefit from a strengthening currency.

The unemployment figures of all major countries are a major trading factor, but perhaps the most important is the **US Non-Farm Payrolls** figure, as the US is the Western cornerstone of global economic growth (the Eastern one is China, of course). This is released by the US Department of Labor Statistics at 8:30am US Eastern time on the first Friday of every month. It estimates the total number of paid workers in the US, excluding those working in: the Government, private household employees, non-profit organisations and farm workers. Together, 'non-farm' employees account for about 80% of US GDP.

As with all figures, major or minor, **it is not so much a case of what the figure actually is or what it means for an economy but rather how it compares to market expectations of what it should be**. Hence, if, as demonstrated below, the market believes that US employment is likely to increase at a certain level but the figure comes in at a level lower than those expectations then that country's currency will fall. The chart below shows the effect of the anticipation that previous estimates that employment conditions would continue to improve significantly were mistaken.

USDCHF (1 Year, Daily)

[Chart Key:

A = release of numbers showing that the rate of recent declines in the US unemployment figures slowed, raising some questions about the sustainability of the US Federal Reserve's intention to continue to taper down its buying of bonds for quantitative easing purposes]

Two problems of which to be aware in trading NFP figures are: first, that they **tend to be revised at various points close to the initial announcement** (and thus, a **false move** is very common – e.g. a move down followed by a move up or vice-versa); and second, **they are released at a time when there are very few major market participants in the market** (London traders are generally down the pub by that time on a Friday, New York traders are probably making their way to their country houses in Connecticut, and Asia is asleep), so these moves **tend to be very violent** one way and then the other.

Moody's		S&P		Fitch		
Long-term	Short-term	Long-term	Short-term	Long-term	Short-term	
Aaa		AAA		AAA		Prime
Aa1		AA+		AA+		High grade
Aa2	P-1	AA	A-1+	AA	F1+	High grade
Aa3		AA-		AA-		
A1		A+		A+		Upper medium grade
A2		A	A-1	A	F1	Upper medium grade
A3	P-2	A-		A-	F2	
Baa1		BBB+	A-2	BBB+		
Baa2	P-3	BBB		BBB		Lower medium grade
Baa3		BBB-	A-3	BBB-	F3	
Ba1		BB+		BB+		Non-investment grade speculative
Ba2		BB		BB		Non-investment grade speculative
Ba3		BB-		BB-		
B1		B+	B	B+	B	
B2		B		B		Highly speculative
B3		B-		B-		
Caa1	Not prime	CCC+				Substantial risks
Caa2		CCC				Extremely speculative
Caa3		CCC-	C	CCC	C	In default with little prospect for recovery
Ca		CC				In default with little prospect for recovery
		C				
C		D	/	DDD	/	In default
/				DD		

Below shows the deleterious effect on the EUR of a four notch (grade) downgrade by Moody's on Greece's foreign currency debt profile, from A3 to Ba1. This pattern has been repeated whenever there is speculation that another of the eurozone's fiscally-challenged members may about to be downgraded. The converse, of course, is true for an upgrade scenario.

EURUSD (5 Years, Weekly)

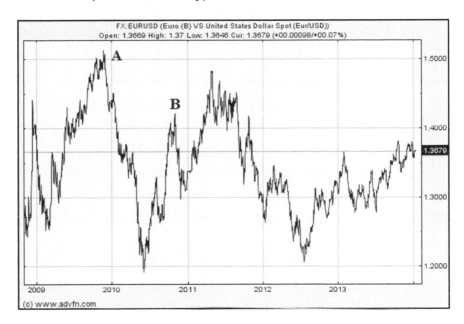

[Chart Key:

A = In October 2009, the newly elected government of Greece revealed that previous Greek governments had been underreporting the country's budget deficit. The underreporting was exposed through a revision of the forecast for the 2009 budget deficit from 6%-8% of GDP (no greater than 3% of GDP was a rule of the Maastricht Treaty that underpinned membership of the eurozone) to 12.7%. Markets learned that Greece's debt was well over EUR400bn and that France owned 10% of that debt, highlighting the risk of bad debt contagion across the Zone and raising questions about other 'weaker' countries in the Zone, including Ireland, Portugal, Italy and Spain, and, by extension, the security and creditworthiness of the entire European banking system.

B = On 23 April 2010, the Greek government requested an initial loan of EUR45bn from the EU and International Monetary Fund (IMF) to cover its financial needs for the remaining part of 2010. A few days later S&P

slashed Greece's sovereign debt rating to BB+ or 'junk' status amid fears of default, in which case investors were liable to lose 30–50% of their money]

Risk Management

The Nature Of Risk

As I mentioned, money ultimately will go to where it is best rewarded for the concomitant risks involved. This is, broadly speaking, the definition of the 'risk curve'. Traders, in order to be successful over time, need to be constantly **aware of this risk curve and also to manage the risk/reward ratio of their own investment portfolio in a logical, sensible and emotionless fashion**. Otherwise, they will go broke. It is as simple as that.

The major mistake that traders make is that they get carried away (i.e. let their heart rule their head) with their running positions. Trading is no place for a heart. If you want to spend your days ruled by emotional swings, take lots of drugs, listen to Nirvana and buy a shotgun. Look what it did for Kurt Cobain.

In the case of in-the-money (ITM) positions, bad traders (i.e. those not managing their risk properly) **exit at the wrong time**, either getting out once the peak profit-taking opportunity has passed (through misplaced greed) or getting nervous and taking profit way before they should.

In the case of out-of-the-money positions (OTM), in the meantime, they **hang on to bad positions** hoping that they will turn around. In this latter case, the only real excuse for this hanging on hopefully is if you have invested in sterling and the Governor of the Bank of England personally called you and swore to you on his children's lives – and with a bible in his other hand – that he will be raising UK interest rates by 20% that afternoon, that the budget deficit has been cut to zero unexpectedly, that new figures to be released in the next 10 minutes will show unemployment at 0%, that inflation is stable at a positive rate and that all of the banks have decided to underwrite a sane economic rebound for the country.

If this is not the case then you are guessing, and you might as well take all of the money out of your trading account and give it to a homeless charity because: a. At least it will do some good for others; and b. It will probably do you some good in the longer-term, as on the streets is precisely where you will end up trading in such a manner.

The Risk Curve

This encapsulates the idea that the more risk involved in a currency which broadly acts – along with bonds and equities – as a proxy for the perceived health of the sovereign country of origin, the more reward (interest rate) is required. Hence, **the worse an economy is perceived to be doing the more reward investors will want as compensation to hold that currency**. And by extension, if that interest rate does not increase then that currency will be unpopular and thus weak.

(For more information, see the previous section on The Risk Curve.)

The Difference Between Probability And Risk/Reward

All other trading training companies of which I am aware commonly use the former term – probability – when they should be discussing the latter, as the two are not the same.

The law of probability (more accurately, the **'Law of Large Numbers'**) is:

"If the probability of a given outcome to an event is P and the event is repeated N times then the larger N becomes, so the likelihood increases that the closer, in proportion, will be the occurrence of the given outcome to N*P."

In practical terms, this means really that if you toss a two-sided coin a sufficient number of times then the distribution of the results between heads coming up and tails coming up will be exactly the same.

Right away, I hope, you can see **a problem here for the trader**. There is a 50/50 chance on the first toss that heads will come up, therefore, according to the logical extension of the other training companies it would be perfectly reasonably to put half your money on heads. You do so, and it comes up tails. Oh dear. Nonetheless, according to the aforementioned rationale, you now put everything on heads coming up, as, given that tails came up first time, and the probability of heads coming up was 50% (1 in 2), heads is bound to come up next time. Does it? Of course not. And now you're broke – remember what I said about giving your money to the homeless?

The fact is that probability only does a part of the way to explaining sequences of numbers (which is what any trading actually is).

There is also the **random walk theory**, in which followers believe that market prices follow a completely random path up and down, without any influence being exerted on them by past price action, making it impossible to predict with any accuracy which direction the market will move at any point or indeed to what degree.

However, as we know, this is plainly incorrect, as patterns of all sorts manifest themselves daily, indeed hourly, and all that is required is to know what to look for.

Risk/reward ratios are what you need to know, and that is what we are coming onto.

Risk/Reward Ratios, Capital Risks And Basic Effective Order Management

Knowing **accurate support and resistance levels is pivotal in determining the risk/reward ratio of a particular trade and in placing orders to capitalise on favourable movements** (take-profit orders) or to limit the downside potential of a trade (stop-loss orders).

Technical Analysis (*see the Technical Analysis section*) is a bit of a self-fulfilling prophecy as whether or not there is any real empirical value in the levels that its classical application produces – the most basic cornerstones being support and resistance levels, as mentioned earlier – the fact that lots of other people believe in it means that these levels take on a trading significance. Frankly, if everybody thought it was cobblers then, in fact, it would not work. Nonetheless, because people like to see patterns in what is effectively chaos, an understanding of Technical Analysis should be an essential part of everybody's trading armoury nowadays.

One distinct advantage that this 'collective delusion of discerning patterns' means on a day to day basis is that, once you have worked out where the key support and resistance levels really are – and this is a pretty straightforward process – and you have set your risk parameters according to your appetite (remember in the early days of trading to go for at least a 1 to 4 risk/reward ratio) then you should place your stop-loss orders appropriately and STOP messing around with your trades UNLESS something major happens that invalidates your original hypotheses for undertaking the trades in the first place.

More money has been lost by people messing around with their trades, or trading through boredom, than has ever been lost in rogue trading operations. If you did the Technical Analysis and all the other things that you should have done before entering a trade, and nothing extraordinary changes – political, economic, Acts of God –

then relax. If you can't relax in front of your screen then leave your orders with your broker/bank/platform and go out to a place where you cannot keep doing daft, unsubstantiated trades because you 'felt like it' or 'were bored' or 'had a hunch' or 'the dog told me to do it'.

USDCAD (4 Years, Weekly)

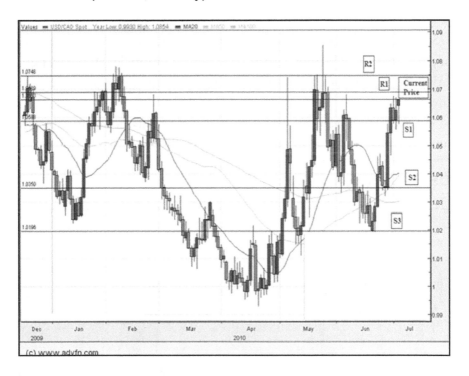

[Chart Key:
R1 = First resistance level, which is 1.0691
R2 = Second resistance level, which is 1.0748
S1 = First support level, which is 1.0588
S2 = Second support level, which is 1.0350
S3 = Third support level, which is 1.0195]

In this context, in the above example, the USDCAD1.0691 R1 level has been a resistance point on four major occasions in the previous six months, whilst there has been only limited support on the S1 level in the same period.

Consequently, if the price neared R1, all other things remaining equal, the preferred strategy would be to sell USD and buy CAD, as the upside loss potential looks capped at the USDCAD1.0691 level, that is 29 pips, whilst the downside gain is likely to be at least 57 pips (to S1) and a break there may signal a further move down to the USDCAD1.0350 S2 level. The downside, though, to the second support level is 238 pips and to the third support level is 312 pips, bringing the overall risk/return ratio to around 11 times in your favour.

In the above example, any risk could be militated against by the judicious **placing of orders**.

USDCAD (4 Years, Weekly)

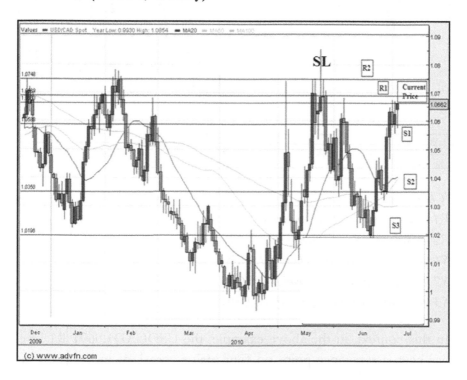

[Chart Key:

*SL = In the chart above, a **stop loss order** (buying back one's short position)*
could be placed just above it at 1.0755, at a potential total loss of £64]

Net Margin/Trading
Requirement (NMR/NTR)

When trading on any platform, an RT will find that his room for manoeuvre in trading is not only limited by the total amount of capital that he has in his trading account but also by the NMR/NTR of that particular platform.

For example, even if not trading on any leverage at all (instead, trading £1 per pip meaning £1 gained/lost for each pip gained/lost), one will find that **for each £1 traded the platform will reduce one's available account balance by anywhere from £100 to £200** or more, depending upon the type of contract that one has entered into (depending on how risky/volatile the platform assesses each contract to be.

Not only will this eat into your available capital but additionally **any losses that a trade occurs as it is ongoing will also be deducted from available capital**.

So, let us say that you have sold EURUSD at 1.3500 at GBP4 per pip. Even before the pair has moved your capital account will be showing that you are down on available capital by, let us say, GBP800. If you had available capital before trading of £1,000 then you can only afford to have the position go 200 pips against you before you are automatically closed out of the position (and thus wiped out entirely) by the trading platform.

Moreover, it affords you **no opportunity for hedging positions** as they run *(see below)*.

Conversely, of course, if your position makes money from the off then your available capital will increase (although this will not affect the amount that the platform has set aside for your risk margin).

Account Size And Setting Targets

To reiterate, in order to have any peace of mind as a trader, one requires an account with sufficient capital for one's trading ambitions. Or, conversely, one needs to have trading ambitions that are cut according to one's capital. One cannot have an imbalance here.

(See the previous section on Account Size And Setting Targets.)

Straight Averaging Up

Given the premise that the aim of trading is to minimise any losses and to maximise any wins, averaging up – if done well – is a good way of achieving the latter.

The basic averaging technique is pretty self-explanatory: it involves adding to your winning position as the trade continues into profitable territory. So, for example, in the chart below, you have entered a new position by buying EUR against the USD (selling USD) at 1.3000 – after your technical analysis, you worked out accurately that a break of this key resistance level would indicate a move higher – and have decided to add £1 per pip at every 50 pip upwards increment. Having done this three times, you now have an average long position of £3 per pip at EURUSD1.3050.

EURUSD (5 Years, Weekly)

[Chart Key:
A = Buy EURUSD at 1.3000, £1 per pip
B = Buy again at 1.3050, £1 per pip
C = Buy again at 1.3100, £1 per pip
D = Therefore, average long price at £3 per pip is 1.3050]

On £1 per pip at 1.3000, one would have made £250 as the EURUSD hit 1.3250. Another £1 per pip at 1.3050 would have netted a further £200 and the final £1 per pip at 1.3100 a further £150. The total, therefore, would have been £600.

Of course, had one put on £3 per pip in the first trade, the profit would have been £750. Additionally the break-even on the trade has now moved up to 1.3050 rather than 1.3000.

If one had not sold at the top of that particular move and the pair had traded down to 1.3100 then one might have lost the third leg profit of £150, which would have resulted in a net profit of just £150.

Also, if the pair had traded back down through the 1.3050 area then one would have incurred a loss on the third long, together with no profit on the second, which would have resulted in a net profit of nothing at all.

Layered Averaging Up

Another way of averaging up that tends against the above phenomenon of being averaged out of any profit is to **add to your long position on pullbacks to the preferred entry level**. So, if you decide to go long as above then you simply add £1 per pip on any move back towards the 1.3000 level, if you are expecting a sustained move upwards over time.

Such tactics are particularly useful if there is an ongoing struggle between a central bank and a fund on two sides of the trade. For example in USDJPY, after the new Prime Minister Shinzo Abe came to power at the end of 2012, the Bank of Japan has been buying USD and selling JPY very aggressively in order to support its export market (and thus aid broader economic recovery) from around the USD85.50 level, whilst certain funds – especially hedge funds – were selling USD and buying JPY anywhere above 87.00.

Once Abe was more firmly ensconced as PM, this battle has moved up the values on USDJPY, as the Bank of Japan was given a much broader policy mandate than before, in line with those given also to the US Fed and the Bank of England, which included looking at employment rates, interest rates and inflation, and in this vein using quantitative easing (QE) where necessary together with direct currency intervention and Forward Guidance as a means of manipulating their respective currencies.

It was only when, in fact, the Bank of Japan was tasked with ensuring a broad-based policy strategy – engineering sustained nominal annual economic growth of 3% (there has been no average annual nominal GDP growth for 15 years) and at least a 2% annual inflation rate every year from 2015, as well as commencing a massive domestic bond-buying QE programme (Fed-style) – that the JPY managed sustained depreciation of the sort wanted by Abe, and moved through the key USDJPY100 resistance level.

Alternately, **adding smaller amounts to the initial position is also a better way in the minds of many to take advantage of further moves** (in the aforementioned case) whilst also limiting the potential – as shown above – for all of one's profits to be eradicated (or even to start making a loss).

The converse of this, of course, is averaging down, in which a trader adds to losing positions in the hopes of making money back quicker as the original position reverses.

Value Averaging

As a natural corollary of the above, value averaging is another added value way of managing positions, this time by constantly readjusting one's risk/reward exposure to a pre-determined level. Therefore, in practical terms, one sets **an amount that falls within one's risk/reward parameters that one wished to have in a particular asset over a particular time**.

For example, one may decide that one wishes to have a total exposure per day of £100 in EURUSD, at £1 per pip. In this event, if the position makes £10 in one day then next day one takes the £10 out and still has £100 riding on the position (at the original price).

Conversely, if the position loses £10 in one day then the following day one would add another £10 at whatever the new price is to compensate. Thus, one has now spent £110 on the long, albeit it a more favourable average, given a downtrading market.

Trailing Stops

As a position turns into profit, the amount of Net Margin Requirement (NMR)/Net Trading Requirement (NTR) that one has available increases, which can be used either for reinvestment in one of the methods detailed above or can be left where it is, depending on the nature of the market at the time.

Nonetheless, depending upon how you manage your position, there is no point in keeping your stop loss exit order at its original point, but rather you should move it up as the profit margin increases, and this is the notion of trailing stops.

So, basically, if your position increases profit by 10 pips then move your stop up 10 pips and so on.

Hedging

A perfect hedge means one in which no risk whatsoever is taken. As a corollary of this, it means that there will also be no reward. The perfect hedge would be, for instance, buying EURUSD 1mn and simultaneously selling EURUSD 1mn. Thus, to me, perfect hedging is a rather pointless exercise.

Instead, I am interested in a broader sort of hedging that can either help reduce my overall net losses in a bad position (by making offsetting gains in other related areas) or help add to my overall net profits (whilst not actually proportionately increasing the risk involved). In this sense, then, hedging is a method of dynamically managing the risk/reward profile for the trader.

Cross-Currency Hedging

Beginning with the bleeding obvious, all currency trades involve buying one currency and selling another.

Let us use EURUSD as the beginning of this example. You are long the EUR, which means you are also short USD: in market code +EURUSD (always mark your position in terms of the base currency first, then the amount (EUR1mn) and then the price (here, 1.5063). Therefore, in market terms you write on your pad: +EURUSD1 @1.5063.)

EURUSD (5 Years, Weekly)

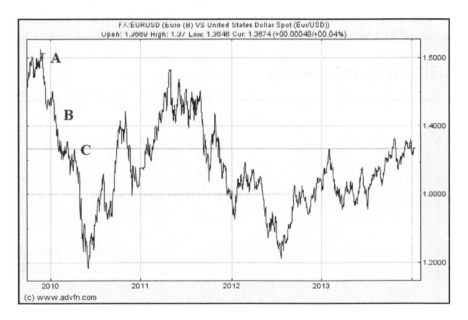

[Chart Key:

A= Buy euros, 1mn and sell US dollars at 1.5063

B = Getting nervous about the euro story, so buy US dollars, 1.5mn and sell Swiss francs at 1.0262

C = I now have options – I am long EURUSD, long USDCHF, making money on the latter going up as the former goes down. Additionally, I can re-

weight positions, depending on how each pairing performs (I can, for example, add to my long USDCHF position or reduce my long EURUSD position) or simply sell EURCHF, as I am effectively net long of that, or I can do counter-balancing stock indices trades]

The market is going against me but I believe (for some good reason) that the EUR will go up soon.

However, I am not exactly sure when and how much the swing against me might be. I know that, by definition, if the EUR element of this pair is going down then the USD element of it is going up.

Therefore, I can go long the USD against something else to attempt to make money on the rising USD as the EUR goes down, so I go long USDCHF1.5mn as EURUSD breaks through the 1.4750 level on 11 December 2009.

USDCHF (5 Years, Weekly)

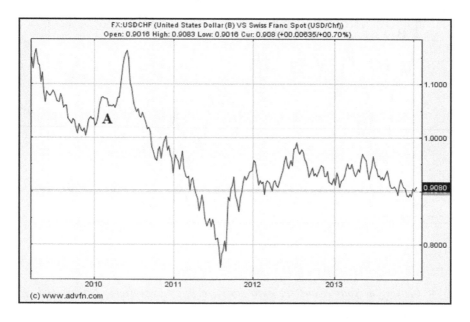

[Chart Key:
A = Buy USD/sell CHF1.5mn at 1.0262]

Now things are looking up (no pun intended), as one is counterbalancing the other almost perfectly, as can be seen from the chart below, given that I am essentially long EURCHF.

As the EUR continues in its downward trend I can use some of the averaging techniques described above to help loss turn into profit.

This is simply a question of re-weighting each trade. As it stands, I have the same overall capital involved in each trade (EUR1mn or around USD1.5mn) but as the EURUSD continues to trade down, I can add to my long USDCHF position. Let us say that I double it, at 1.0400 to USD3mn for the entire duration of the downtrend in EURUSD, which continues until the beginning of June.

Looking at these trades in P&L terms then:

+EURUSD1mn @ 1.5063, liquidate at 1.1800 = total loss of EUR326,300 (= USD at the new rate = USD385,034).

+USDCHF1mn @ 1.0262, liquidate at 1.1700 = USD143,800

and +USDCHF2mn @ 1.0400, liquidate at 1.1700 = USD260,000.

Therefore, my total profit for the venture (which did not start out well) was USD77,500.

EURCHF (5 Years, Weekly)

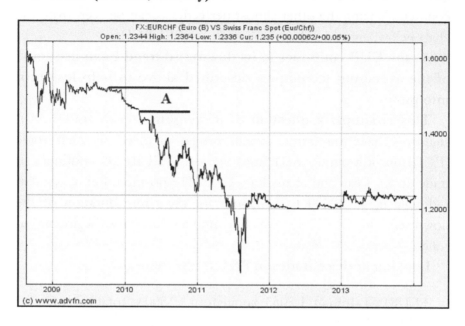

[*Chart Key:*

A = *Overall, with just a flat long EURCHF position I am only down 250-300 pips but I can get rid of this entirely by re-weighting*]

In the above example, I could also have sold EURCHF, which would have given me a flat position, as:

1. +EUR – USD

2. +USD – CHF

3. Therefore, net long EURCHF.

4. Therefore, sell EURCHF = flat.

However, there were many **other options available** to me whilst I was long EURUSD and long USDCHF:

1. **Increase the relative weighting of the long USDCHF position** (as described above) or I could think more laterally still and **buy the USD against something else as well**.

2. This would have increased my net long USD position but also it would have allowed me to **insulate myself against any CHF-specific good news** that might cause it to rally and thus lose me money on my long USDCHF position – for example, if the central bank of Switzerland (SNB) raised interest rates unexpectedly or whatever.

3. Therefore, I would have looked around for **other currencies where the outlook was grim** and good news was not expected on the horizon. At the time, GBP looked especially ropey, with an unpopular government still in power but no clear successor likely to prevail in the General Elections, bad economic numbers, consumer spending still low, housing prices stymied and so on, so I could have sold GBP and bought USD.

4. This again could be reweighted in terms of amount.

5. And so the process goes on.

Cross-Asset Class Hedging

Sticking with my failing long EURUSD position example for the time being, I need not have just hedged my bets with currencies.

Let us recap on the basic situation: I had gone long EUR, expecting some turnaround in the fortunes of the currency, based perhaps on the notion that future figures might show that the weaker eurozone members (Greece, Spain, Portugal, Italy, Ireland) might be turning themselves around.

So, what else could I do to capitalise on the continued poor performance of the eurozone that is crucifying my long EURUSD position?

1. Sell the major stock indices associated with the individual countries performing especially badly in the EUR region (as shown above).

Greece Athens Stock Exchange (5 Years, Weekly)

Had I sold the ASE as above, say another USD1mn worth my entry price at the time would have been around 2250 and falling fast.

I could also have sold the other major indices of troubled eurozone countries.

2. Looking at it another way, I could have bought US stock indices instead/as well as.

Dow Jones Industrial Average (5 Years, Weekly)

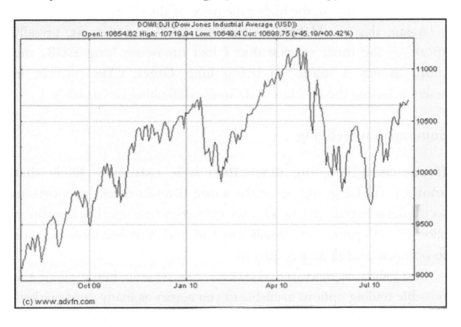

3. If I was, in the meantime, suddenly concerned about my net short CHF position then I could hedge out the CHF risk, by buying the major Swiss stock index.

4. I could have done a currency option to hedge risks either side (we will discuss options later on).

Cross-Sovereign/Credit Rating Hedging

Given that the credit risk for the troubled eurozone members was increasing over the period when the EUR was falling out of bed, I could buy **credit default swaps** (CDS) on the countries worst affected. **CDS are basically like insurance policies on entities going bankrupt** (for example companies or, in this case, countries) – the more technical definition is: CDS pay the buyer face value in exchange for the underlying securities or the cash equivalent should a government or company fail to adhere to its debt agreements. The higher the likelihood, the higher the price of the CDS.

Again, this would have hedged my EUR exposure as, broadly speaking, **the more money that I lost on being long EUR, the more money I made on being long Greek CDS** (that is, in essence, buying the likelihood of Greece defaulting on its debt).

Summary on Hedging

If one asset is going down then it is extremely likely that another will be going up at the same time in direct proportion, so thinking laterally about all asset markets when one has a position allows you to get out of virtually any bad trade that you have made or to optimise profits on a good one.

Preferably, as discussed elsewhere, you should know all of the possible trading options available to you across as many asset markets as possible before you enter into the trade in the first place.

Options

An option is the right, but not the obligation, to buy or sell an asset at a particular price (the exercise price) on or before a specific future date (the exercise date).

The two most common types of option are called an **American** style option (which can be exercised at any point up to the option expiration date) and a **European** style option (which can only be exercised on the specific exercise date).

(For the more 'exotic' Asian options the payoff is determined by the *average underlying price over some pre-set period of time*, conceptually different from both the American and European option types in which in both cases the payoff of the option contract depends on the *price of the underlying instrument at exercise*.)

An **option to buy an asset is called a call option** and an **option to sell one is called a put option.**

You can buy or sell an option.

If you **sell an option then you receive a premium** from the buyer (a bit like an insurance premium), however, you are obligated as the seller to pay out to the buyer in the event that the option is exercised (and these payouts can be limitless, depending on how the option has moved).

Options are extremely useful as hedging tools (this was their original purpose, as a type of insurance against unforeseen movements in asset prices) but, as with all financial assets, they can also be used for purely aggressive speculative purposes.

In a currency option, then – let us stick with the EURUSD example that we have been predominantly using in the last few pages – if you bought a EURUSD call then you would be buying the right (but not the obligation) to buy EUR and sell USD, and if you bought a EURUSD put then you would be buying the right (but not the obligation) to sell EUR and buy USD.

And vice-versa if you were selling a call or put – you have a liability then to meet the obligation implied in the option if the buyer decides to exercise it.

Although we are not going to go into huge details about the pricing of options, one thing that it is useful to be aware of is that **the premium paid to buy an option is a reflection both of the exercise price of the option (and whether it is currently in profit, ITM or out of profit, OTM, *see above*) and also the volatility of the market for the currency pair.**

Looking at options in terms of them being insurance policies is quite helpful in a number of regards.

Let us say that you have bought a house and you want to insure its contents against theft for £10,000. The insurance company has to decide on a range of factors in determining the level of your premiums. Have you got window and door locks, are you backing onto a secluded area, is it an area known for burglaries etc? So, let us say that the answers are: yes to locks, no to secluded area, no to burglaries. The insurance company decides that overall you will have to pay them only their £10,000 back over 20 years. This implies zero risk volatility or thereabouts.

One year in, and there are a spate of burglaries in the area. You premiums go up. This is increasing risk volatility and so on and so forth. You have a private security firm patrolling your grounds 24/7, so your premiums go down again due to lower risk volatility.

In the EURUSD example, the player had gone long EUR short USD at 1.5063, and the position had started to go against him almost from the off.

The near-perfect hedge here would have been to buy a EURUSD put (the right but not the obligation to sell EUR and buy USD) at a strike price of 1.5063 although the price would have to be adjusted slightly to take into account the premium that the player would have paid to the seller of the option, but basically you get the idea.

He could, conversely, have banked money in advance if he had sold a EURUSD call option (giving someone the right but not the obligation to buy EUR from the player, therefore the player is selling them and buying USD) also at 1.5063.

There are more interesting ways to actually make money from options, of course, by locking in certain profit zones through a combination of buying and selling calls and puts at different prices, taken together with different hedging techniques, but for the RT it is not especially something they should be considering I would say, certainly not in the first few phases of his development.

Technical Analysis

Candlesticks

This method of charting is particularly useful as it not only shows simply whether the market has largely bought the base currency (typically shown in green or white) or sold it (typically shown in red or black) but also how strong these buys or sells were (indicated by the length of the lines above each candle, **'wick'**, for buying or below, **'shadow'**, for selling).

Candlestick Structure

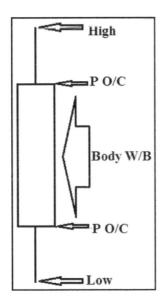

[Chart Key:
High = Highest price during trading time period
P O/C = Trading time period open or close price

Body W/B = Real body is white (or green) if currency closed higher over the trading period or black (or red) if it closed lower
P O/C = Trading time period open or close price
Low = Lowest price during trading time period]

If a market is undecided as to where it views the direction of a pair then the candlestick will have no substantial body, wick or shadow (**'doji'**), reflecting that the price closed the day where it opened and that neither buyers ('bulls') nor sellers ('bears') prevailed in moving the pair their way over the course of the trading hours.

A similar inference can be taken from the **'Spinning Top'** pattern, although not to quite the same degree, as some intra-day movement will have taken place. In either event, both can be viewed as **marking possibly the end of the previous trend**, as it has run out of steam. These patterns make ideal places to enter new trades or exit existing ones.

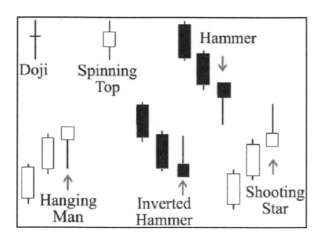

The **'Hammer'** pattern appears after a previous move to the downside and indicates that a move to the upside is on the cards. The long shadow shows that, despite it trading substantially lower during the day, the weight of selling was not sufficient for it to stay at depressed trading levels. Consequently, the inference is that major buyers have stepped in at these levels and may well continue buying overnight or as the new Western trading period properly commences.

The same can be said for the '**Inverted Hammer**', although to a lesser degree, as, although buyers have stepped into the market, they have failed, on this occasion, to reverse the downtrend entirely.

Conversely, the '**Shooting Star**' should be read as a sign that a move to the downside is on the cards, after a previous move to the upside, with bulls having failed to continue to push the pair higher and substantial bears having now entered the market.

The same can be said for the '**Hanging Man**' although to a lesser degree, as, although sellers have stepped into the market, they have failed, on this occasion, to reverse the uptrend entirely.

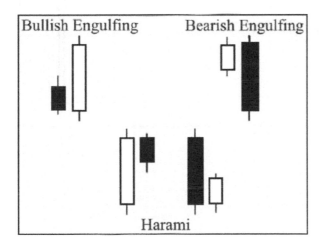

A '**Bullish Engulfing**' pattern is a clear indication that the signs of reversal of a previous trend (either through a Shooting Star or Hanging Man) have gained momentum, and the reverse is true of the '**Bearish Engulfing**' pattern (either through the Hammer or Inverted Hammer).

The '**Harami**' pattern, though, which can occur either after a move up or down, can be taken again as a sign of uncertain price follow-through and may mark the beginning of a change of trend direction.

USDCAD (1 Year, Daily)

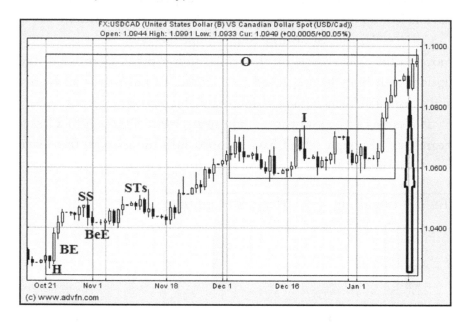

[Chart Key:
H = Hammer
BE = Bullish engulfing
SS = Shooting star
BeE = Bearish engulfing
STs = Spinning tops
O = Overall uptrend
I = Indecision of the market]

In all of the above cases, the **weight that one should attach to these patterns should be increased when additional confirmations are found.**

These can be where they occur at **major resistance and support levels, Fibonacci levels** (key mathematical ratios of an original

number, representing a move up or down: 23.6%, 38.2%, 50% and
61.8%) or **Moving Average** levels (simply, each day's price added
together and then divided by a certain number of days: 20, 50 and
100 are the most used), including selected oscillators.

In the above chart, for instance, aside from a few moves down
(which fail to gather momentum, as indicated by the Spinning Top
patterns) all of the significant moves have been to the upside (as
indicated by the rolling Hammer patterns).

USDCAD (1 Year, Daily)

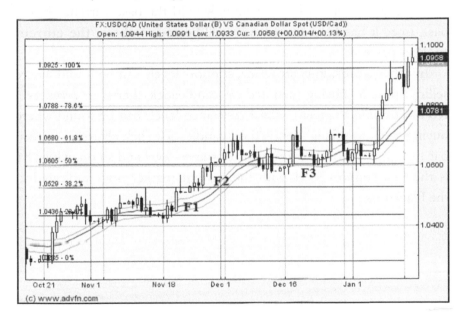

[Chart Key:
F1 = Fibonacci level 1, 23.6%
F2 = Fibonacci level 2, 38.2%
F3 = Fibonacci level 3, 50.0%]

Interestingly here, though, it can be seen that the Moving Averages
and the Fibonacci levels have acted both as support and resistance
levels at various times throughout the trading cycle, and where these

have occurred concomitant with the candlestick patterns as described above, they have led to a sustained move in whichever direction they pointed.

Resistance And Support Levels

Support levels (where the market has overwhelmingly bought the base currency in the past, once it has been in decline) will invariably be found **below the current market price**, whilst **resistance levels** (where the market has overwhelmingly sold the base currency in the past, once it has been on the rise) will be found **above the current market price**.

In other words, in chart terms, support levels can be found where selling turns to buying (denoted on candlestick charts, *see below*, as a red bar turning to green), whilst resistance levels can be found where buying turns to selling (denoted on candlestick stick charts as a green bar turning to red). R1 is the first resistance level and so on, whilst S1 is the first support level, with the current market price indicated in the black box.

EURUSD (1 Year, Daily)

FX:EURUSD (Euro (B) VS United States Dollar Spot (Eur/USD))
Open: 1.3678 High: 1.3679 Low: 1.3579 Cur: 1.3588 (-00.00897/-00.66%)

[Chart Key:
S1 = First support level
S2 = Second support level
R1 = First resistance level
R2 = Second resistance level]

These levels should be the cornerstones of all serious trading activity, as they act (together with other confirmations, discussed below) as signals to buy or sell into a new position or to exit existing ones.

To reiterate, though, **it is essential to note that resistance and support levels do not always coincide with any/all of these additional confirmation signals**. It may well be, for example, that a particular level has been **targeted by a country's central bank** as being essential for the advancement of its economic or monetary policy and that it will act decisively to ensure either that its currency weakens at a certain level (to encourage exports and boost economic growth, for instance) or strengthens (to discourage demand-led inflation, for instance).

The chart below, for example, shows the determination of the Bank of Japan (always one of the more active global central banks) stepping in to prevent the JPY from strengthening to such a degree that the country's exports would become even more uncompetitive in the world's markets than already was the case at the time.

USDJPY (5 Years, Weekly)

[Chart Key:
R1 to R10 = The sequentially lower resistance levels hit by serious hedge funds and others, from longs taken out all the way down, before the Bank of Japan effectively set a floor]

Similarly, it may be that there are enormous **FX options** that would be triggered if a currency reached a certain level. In this case, whomever held the option would do everything cost-effective that they could to prevent it reaching the strike price for the option.

For example, Nick Leeson's problem and the demise of Barings can be attributed entirely to his desire to keep all of the options he had sold (if one sells an option then one receives a premium for that, cash in hand pretty much, but if it reaches the strike price then one is liable to pay out on the options to the option holders – buyers) on the Nikkei. In that case, he had to keep it above the 20,000 mark but unfortunately for him, the Kobe earthquake occurred in Japan, causing the Nikkei to plummet.

He had sold billions of GBP-worth of options and netted the premiums to use to cover up other smaller trading losses that his team had made, so he had to keep propping up the market by buying Nikkei futures contracts, in order not to have to pay out on these options. These, by the way, were put options on the Nikkei – that is, they allowed people who bought them the right but not the obligation to sell the Nikkei at or before a certain date (call options are the right to buy a particular asset on or before a certain date).

In Leeson's case, this meant that he could be faced with vast numbers of buyers of these put options exercising their right to sell the Nikkei to Leeson at 12,000 and immediately being able to buy it back at around 15,000 – a massive profit for them and an equally massive loss for him, so he had little option (no pun intended) but to buy the Nikkei. This made it not worth the while of these put options buyers to exercise their options (there is no point in being able to sell it at 20,000 if you can only sell it at 20,000).

Often, one will see levels that apparently have little or no other obvious significance being resolutely defended up to a certain date (the expiration date for the option) and then dramatically going through that level once the option has lapsed, as shown below.

USDCAD (5 Years, Daily)

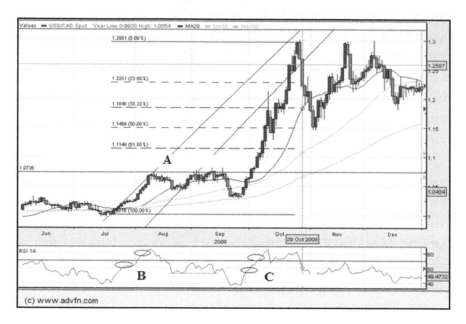

[Chart Key:
A = USD call, CAD put option @ 1.0745
B = Big buying but capped
C = Big buying not capped]

Fibonacci Levels

These are key mathematical ratios of an original number (price), representing a move up or down: **23.6%, 38.2%, 50% (not actually a Fibonacci ratio, but most Fibonacci users include it anyhow), 61.8% and 100%.**

These can be overlaid on a chart, from the bottom of a trend to the top in a bullish market or from the top of a trend to the bottom in a bearish one.

As mentioned earlier, they can often mark resistance and support levels, as shown below.

US Dow Jones Industrial Average (5 Years, Weekly)

[PIC – chart 26.jpg]

[Chart Key:
A = 23.6% Fib level acts as support
B = 38.2% Fib level acts as resistance
C = 50% Fib level acts first as support and then as resistance]

In the above chart, we see clearly the **correlation between Fibonacci levels and those of support and resistance**. Interestingly here we also see that at the 50% level, initially this starts out as a resistance but then, as the cycle progresses, it acts as a support.

Moving Averages

These are particularly useful in determining short-term indications as to whether a market is set to continue in its current trend, reverse that trend or trade in a range. As mentioned earlier, MAs are simply each day's price added together and then divided by a certain number of days: 20, 50 and 100 are the most used.

As an additional confirmation (to established support and resistance levels, for instance), they offer a good idea of whether a currency is likely to break to the topside or the downside, as illustrated below.

USDJPY (5 Years, Weekly)

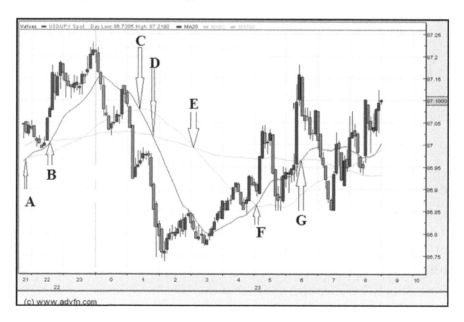

[Chart Key =
A = MA20 up through MA50 = BUY
B = MA20 through MA100 = BUY

C = MA20 down through MA50 = SELL
D = MA20 down through MA 100 = SELL
E = MA50 down through MA100 = OVERSOLD
F = MA20 up through MA100 = BUY
G = MA20 through MA50 = BUY]

Broadly speaking, as shown above, if the short-term MA20 breaks through a longer-term MA then one might expect the currency pair to trade in whichever direction that break has occurred. More helpfully still, MAs can be used for earlier trading indications, using the **Moving Average Convergence-Divergence** (MACD) indicator, as shown below.

USDJPY (5 Years, Weekly)

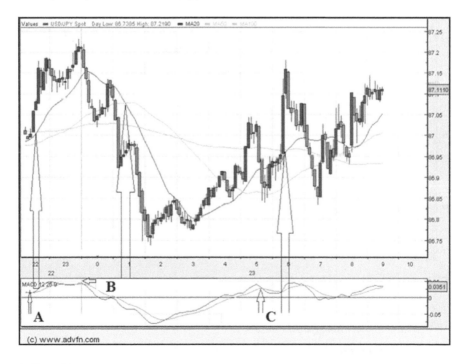

(c) www.advfn.com

[Chart Key:
A = Early signal for crossover = BUY

B = Early signal for crossover = SELL
C = Early warning for crossover = BUY]

MAs are also a vital part of determining the momentum of a price movement, in its application with the 3/10 Oscillator. This is a simple indicator constructed by subtracting the 10 day period Exponential Moving Average from the 3 day period Exponential Moving Average (but, do not fret, virtually all charting packages allow one to replicate this with the MACD by setting the short term parameter to 3, the long term parameter to 10 and the smoothing parameter to 1.

Dow Jones Price/Oscillator Convergence/Divergence Signals

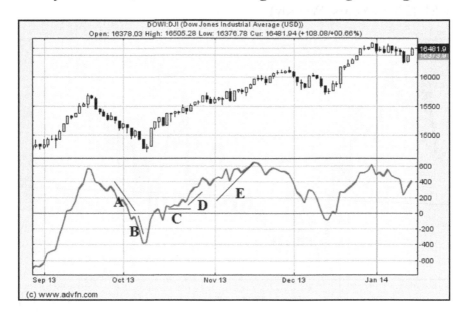

[Chart Key:
A = Selling momentum gathers force
B = Selling momentum diverges = change of direction due
C = Range trading momentum
D = Buying momentum kicks in

E = Buying momentum gathers force]

Anyhow, the concept underlying this indicator (similar in theory to the RSI) is that if a price move up or down is expected to be sustained then one would anticipate that, along with a range of higher highs (for an upmove) or lower lows (for a downmove), the momentum (or force) behind each of these would also be sustained. If not, one would have to question whether the move can have the strength (more buyers than sellers or the other way around) to continue.

Dow Jones Bearish Regular Divergence Of Price/Oscillator

= Although the price is rising, momentum is going down = bearish divergence

[Chart Key:
A = Higher high
B= Lower high]

Dow Jones Bearish Hidden Divergence Of Price/Oscillator

= The price is still bid, but at a lower level, and momentum is gaining at lower prices

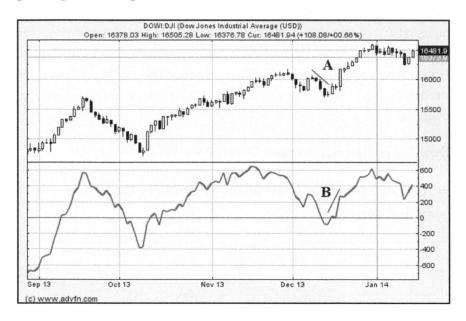

[Chart Key:
A = Lower high
B = Higher high]

Dow Jones Bullish Regular Divergence Of Price/Oscillator

= *Although the price is falling, there is less momentum pushing it down*

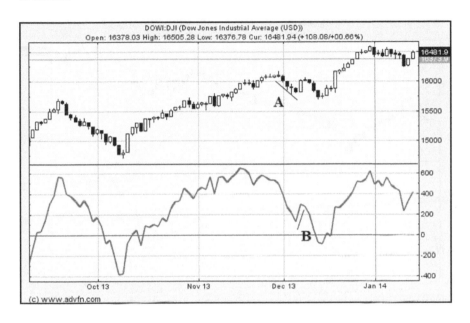

[Chart Key:
A = Lower low
B = Higher low]

Dow Jones Bullish Hidden Divergence Of Price/Oscillator

= Although it is still offered, the momentum gains as the price rises relatively

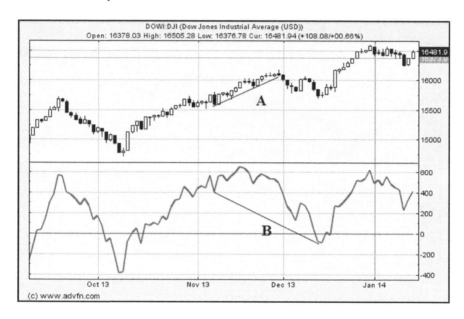

[*Chart Key:*
A = Higher low
B = Lower low]

Relative Strength Index (RSI)

RSI is another extremely useful oscillator indicator. **In general terms, the RSI shows the momentum of a pair's trading – in effect, the degree of market participation in its current price movement – and can act as a valuable pre-emptive indicator showing a potential reversal of trend.**

For example, even if a pair appears to be rising quickly, if the RSI is showing that negative momentum is occurring then it might be time to look at the other indicators that signalled a long position and look to either exit an existing long or establish a new short.

Conversely, as shown in the chart below, there is a very notable shift upwards in RSI higher before the actual market price follows it.

EURUSD (1 Year, Daily)

= RSI confirms upward trend before actual price turns higher

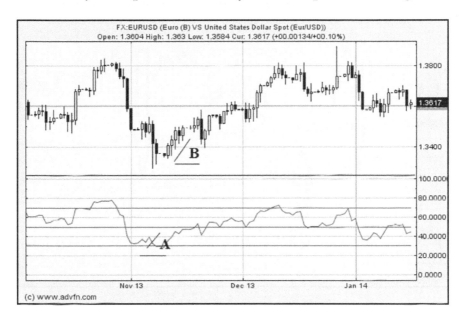

[Chart Key:
A = RSI rises sharply higher, in advance of the price movement
B = Actual market price catches up with bullish momentum on RSI]

More specifically, the RSI moves between a scale of 0 to 100, with 100 showing that every participant in the market is buying the base currency of a pair and 0 showing the opposite. **As a rule of thumb, any reading of 70 and above indicates that the pair is overbought, with a possible reversal on the cards, and any reading under 30 showing it is oversold and that the opposite is**

true. This, together with the formations of usual double top/bottom patterns, can show up even before they do in the actual price movement ('Divergence').

Similarly, areas of support and resistance show up very clearly on RSI patterns, as shown below.

EURUSD (1 Year, Daily)

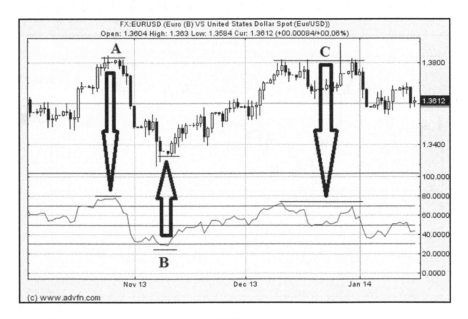

[Chart Key:

A = RSI shows genuine resistance level in the price, in advance

B = RSI shows genuine support level in the price, in advance

C = RSI shows genuine rolling resistance level]

As is evident from the above, RSI's principal use is not in already trending markets, in which it can be used as a confirmation of direction or as an early warning indicator of a change of direction (if above 70 or below 30) but rather in range-bound markets looking for direction.

Here, as shown above, it can act as a proxy for volume interest in particular positions, so that, for example, a sharp spike up in RSI in a market trading around the mid-level could be taken as an early signal of a bullish move and vice-versa.

Bollinger Bands

Right up front I should say that, personally, I am not a big fan of these, but some people set some store by them, so I thought that I should cover them. So, here we go.

Bollinger bands are plotted an equal distance either side of a simple moving average. The default settings on trading programmes use a 20 period simple moving average with the upper band (UB) plotted 2 standard deviations above the moving average and the lower band (LB) plotted 2 standard deviations below it.

In periods of low price volatility, these standard deviations become smaller (this process is called a 'squeeze' in Bollinger parlance) than in periods of high volatility and vice-versa (a 'bubble').

Given this, there is undoubtedly money to be made from anticipating/participating in such a breakout/breakdown to the existing bands.

EURUSD (1 Year, Daily)

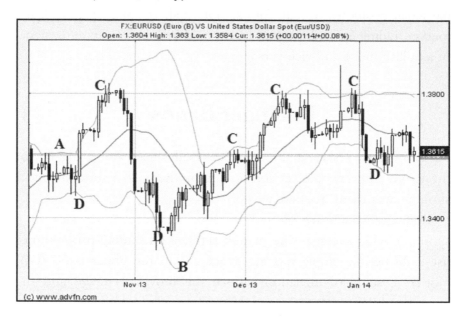

[Chart Key:
A = Squeeze
B = Bubble
C = Upper band acts as resistance level
D = Lower band acts as support level]

More appositely, it is better to use Bollinger bands together with other firmer indicators such as support and resistance levels, Fibonacci levels and so forth, and to use them in such a way as to modify the results with what the Bollinger bands tell you about the probability of a move continuing/reversing.

If the price is moving towards the top of a band then beware longs, and if it is moving towards the bottom of a band then beware shorts. But don't get too hung up on what Bollinger Bands say in and of themselves.

Elliott Wave Theory

The market consists broadly of two types of investors: **institutional ones (huge) and retail ones (small)**. The general parameters of this investment universe are simple enough: in 2009, it was measured that retail traders (RT) on average are responsible for about USD110bn in currency flows across options, swaps, futures and spot forex in total per day; the figure for institutional investors (II), though, was around USD3.2trn, and although the total turnover figure increased in the 2013 BIS FX Survey, the counterparty proportions remained essentially the same.

It is against this backdrop that Elliot Wave Theory is particularly useful as it shows major moves and minor ones, with the former likely to be caused by IIs (and well worth following, if they are not spoofs) and the latter likely to be caused by RTs playing catch-up (normally a good time to start thinking about exiting a trade).

In its most basic form, Elliott Waves show that the market does not move in a completely chaotic fashion but rather is a product of patterns that repeat themselves over time. These patterns ('waves') define a trend, which can be the basis for predictive trading.

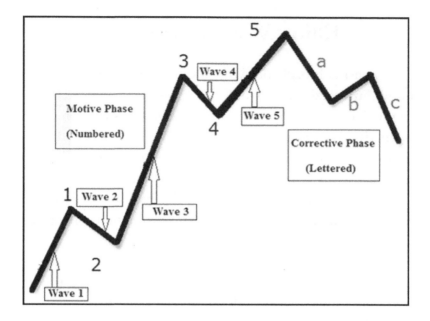

More specifically, according to Elliott (Ralph Nelson Elliott, just in case you were wondering, who posited his theory in around 1934), a trending market moves in a **five-three wave** pattern, where the first five waves ('motive waves') move in the direction of the larger trend. Following the completion of the five waves in one direction, a larger corrective move takes place in three consecutive waves ('corrective waves'), as illustrated in the above chart.

Interestingly, **the patterns identified by Elliott occur across multiple time frames**: that is, a completed five wave sequence on a small time frame (5 minutes, for instance) may well be just the first wave a longer temporal sequence (in a daily chart, for example) and so on and so forth.

Elliott Waves On EURUSD

[Chart Key:
W1 to W5 = Motive phase waves
A to c = Corrective phase waves]

The **combination of Elliott Waves and Fibonacci ratios is particularly useful in trading into new positions or trading out of existing ones for a number of reasons,** outlined as follows: Fibonacci ratios are usually important levels of supply and demand (ie, support and resistance).

The motive and corrective levels are often measured by percentages of the previous wave length, with the most common levels being the Fibonacci ones of 38%, 50%, 61.8% and 100%; timings with a distance of 13, 21, 34, 55, 89 and 144 periods should be particularly monitored (eg, if you find a crucial reversal or an unfolding of a pattern on a daily chart then expect another crucial unfolding at the above daily points thereafter); a corrective move that follows a motive move from a significant low or high usually retraces 50% to 61.8% of the preceding impulse; wave 4 usually corrects as far as 38.2% of wave 3; given that wave 2 generally does not overlap the start of wave 1 (ie, the 100% of it), the start of wave 1 is an ideal level to place stops; and the target of wave 5 can be calculated by multiplying the length of wave 1 by 3.236 (2 X 1.618).

Continuation Patterns

These patterns allow the trader not only to understand from where the price action and momentum has come but also to anticipate where and to what degree it is headed. Thus, as these patterns are also watched by thousands of other traders around the globe, they allow an RT to obtain an ongoing record of the sentiment surrounding a currency pair at any given time and consequently allow the trader to manage his order placing better as well.

Ascending And Descending Triangles

Triangles basically allow the trader to gauge which of the myriad support and resistance levels on a chart are the ones he should be watching most carefully in determining false or genuine breakouts.

An **ascending triangle** is formed by a combination of diagonal support and horizontal resistance, implying that the bulls are gaining the upper hand in the ongoing trading dynamic of the pair and buying at higher and higher levels, while the bears are merely trying to defend an established level of resistance.

EURGBP (1 Year, Daily) Ascending Triangle

[Chart Key:
A = Horizontal resistance level
B = Inclining support]

Clearly, in the above example, the trader has advanced warning that the pair is more likely to break up through the resistance level than down through the support one. Also, of course, by anticipating the formation of the triangle the trader can gain/not lose further points, depending on his position, as currency pairs often trend, consolidate and then re-trend.

In the case of a **descending triangle**, the bears are gaining strength and selling at lower and lower levels, while the bulls are merely trying to defend an established level of support.

AUDUSD (1 Year, Daily) Descending Triangle

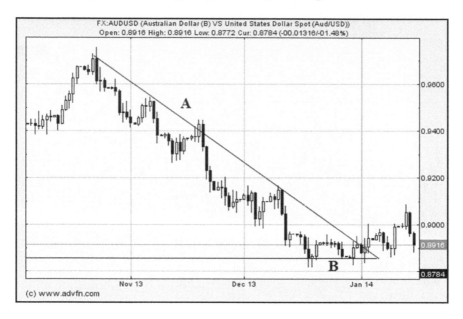

[Chart Key:
A = Declining resistance
B = Horizontal support]

Given these two scenarios, it is easy to see that one can make money rising the principal wave up or down respectively and also to see that triangles make the placement of stop loss orders relatively simple as well; in the ascending triangle example, they would be placed just under the inclining support line at a level that accorded with one's own risk/reward ratio for a rolling long position.

Conversely, in the descending triangle example, they would be placed at a point above the declining resistance level that accorded with one's own risk/reward ratio for a rolling short.

In the cases of both ascending and descending triangles, **any true break (more than one spoof break-out) of its direction (up for descending triangles, down for ascending ones) should be** taken seriously by traders to consider exiting trades made on the trend until that point (taking profit) and reversing positions.

Flags

Flags and pennants generally represent a pause in trend and can be used either to take profits on a position going with that trend or to add to that trending position, if one is feeling particularly aggressive (and, preferably, has one's confidence bolstered by other factors meriting an increase in position size – more favourable than expected fundamental or political developments, for example).

The example below is of a downward trending USDJPY, which pauses for consolidation in a flag pattern, before resuming its downward trajectory. Often one can expect pretty much the same number of pips in the second part of the downtrend (labelled 'Downtrend 2' in the chart, appositely enough) as in the first part of the downtrend (you can work out what this one is labelled), but in the chart below, it seems on cursory glance that this is not the case.

However, looking further into the distance and going on the basis of a longer-term trade, it becomes apparent that, in fact, the real second wave (or you could term it 'Downtrend 2, Part 2) makes up the entire pips expected as a result of Downtrend 1.

USDJPY (5 Years, Weekly) Flag In A Downtrend

[Chart Key:
A = Downtrend 1 = 723 pips
F = Flag
B = Downtrend 2 = 348 pips, OR DOES IT? See Below]

In fact, this flag and many similar presage a much sharper move down, as can be seen below.

USDJPY (5 Years, Weekly) Extended Continuation In A Downtrend

[Chart Key:
F = Flag from previous chart
A = Logical conclusion of the original downtrend 1 = 700 pips had the trade been stuck with]

Trend Reversals – Double Top/Bottom And Head And Shoulders Patterns

Given that the market has a way of generally correcting any untoward excessive movements one way or another in asset prices over time, spotting a real reversal in a trend from just a shimmering mirage is key to making money on a long-term basis.

In this respect, we have already covered a lot of ground, but there are a couple of other, more basic patterns that a trader should look out for.

A **Double Top is, as it sounds, when prices stop rising at the same point twice in a short sequence of time,** as shown below. In order for a real reversal of trend to be indicated, the pair must break down through the key support level as indicated on the chart. This is sometimes the result, as we have also touched on, of a central bank looking to halt the appreciation of its currency to such a degree that its export revenue is damaged (or, indeed, of financial institutions guarding a level in order not to be hit by an option being exercised).

GBPUSD (1 Year, Weekly) Double Top

[Chart Key:
R = Rising trend
T1 = First top
T2 = Second (double) top
S = Break below this double support level here implies downtrend]

A double bottom is the same principle, only reversed.

In the meantime, a head and shoulders pattern, as illustrated below, develops with the exchange rate trending up and forming the left shoulder on a reversal. Then the market trends higher to form the head and falls back to the same support of the first shoulder to form the right shoulder. The neckline is thus the line connecting the troughs between the peaks. If it is broken, expect a downside move to occur.

AUDUSD (1 Year, Daily) Head And Shoulders Trend Reversal Pattern

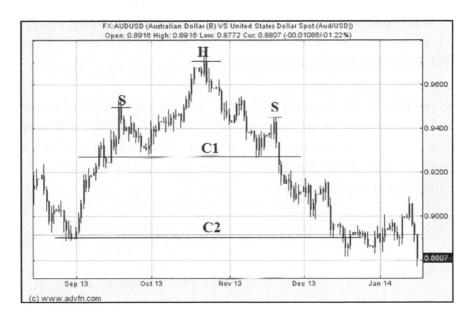

[Chart Key:
S = Shoulder
H = Head
C1 = Confirmation of break down 1
C2 = Confirmation of further breakdown 2]

Summary

Develop your own set of key indicators that you have learnt to combine in such a way that you can trust yourself to interpret them sufficiently well to make money more often that you lose it.

Do not stick every available indicator on a chart, as you will just confuse yourself and lose money.

Personally, despite having done this for over 20 years, I consider a likely winning trade as having as many as possible of the **'Perfect Seven'** attributes which were listed previously *(see the section on Developing A Rigorous And Sound Personal Trading Metholology.)*

With this backdrop in place, manage orders sensibly. Decide where the stop-loss should be (based on one's own risk/reward ratio) and where the take-profit should be (based on one's own risk/reward ratio) and stick to them.

Sticking to whatever methodology one has, provided it is sound, and to one's order levels (and thus risk/reward ratio levels) will mean that one has more free time away from just sitting staring at a screen, that one will make money over time and that one will not go completely bonkers.

Equities' Specifics

A More Regulated Marketplace

Unlike FX, bonds or commodities, the equities market is extremely highly regulated by a range of authorities around the world, although perhaps particularly so in the UK and the USA.

This implies that **it is less prone to the type of sudden hijackings of pricing that occur in the other aforementioned markets**. It also means that virtually all traders, professional or otherwise, are making their decisions based on the same key information, which is – theoretically at least – all publicly available.

Consequently, **equities investment offers retail investors an excellent opportunity to trade on a more level playing field** than a number of other markets and is often a more straightforward story-driven marketplace than FX, bonds or commodities.

That said, all of the **key investment considerations that we have highlighted in our other courses – pertaining to** *Risk Management, Technical Analysis, Psychology of Trading* **and** *Trading Fundamentals* **– are just as important** to adhere to when trading equities as when dealing in any other asset class.

In looking at a selection of the various key equities investment styles to begin with, a useful **analogy would be that of shooting a home movie on a video camera**: the opening shot might be a wide-angle of a street (top-down trading), then the angle is narrowed to the door of a particular house (bottom-up trading), then to the inhabitants inside (management-focussed trading considerations) and then to one particular tight angle shot (key investment ratios).

Top-Down Trading

This is an investment approach that involves **looking at the big picture** (a wide-angle, using our analogy), beginning with the **area** in which a country is located, then the **economic and political dimensions of that country** including **where it is in the business cycle**, then the various **sectors of the economy** and then the **specific details pertaining to a target company** including management and key investment numbers and ratios.

A number of the greatest stock investors in history have used this style of trading to outperform all others in the market, and we shall look at some of them as we proceed, but using George Soros and his partner Jim Rogers in their early days at Soros Fund Management is as good an example as any that I can think of.

Area-Specific Top-Down Trading (Positive Paradigm Shifts)

Basically, when they first began, whilst George was working through the numbers on his computer, Jim would be zooming around the world on his motorbike (later recalled in his book 'Investment Biker' – a very good read for those looking to invest in stocks in a Top-Down style, by the way, and I receive no kickbacks for this recommendation) attempting to spot small changes at ground level in countries that were possibly on the cusp of major changes, through seeing tiny changes in general economic behaviour.

For example, typically this might involve Jim stopping off at a cafe in Hungary in the early 1990s and noticing that the locals were suddenly happy to spend a dollar (equivalent) on a cappuccino.

Hungary: Budapest Stock Exchange (BUX) After Leaving USSR

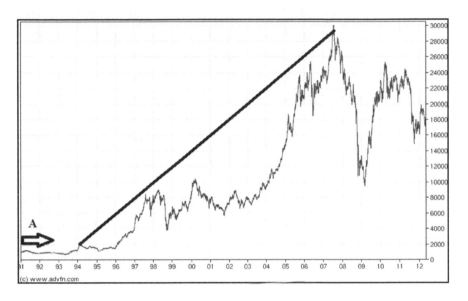

[Chart Key:
A = Straight line constant price of BUX during transition phase from leaving the USSR]

In Jim's mind this indicated the following rationale: people have more money to spend on small luxuries following Hungary's departure from the umbrella of the USSR in 1989 – therefore, people are earning more money as a whole – therefore, people are being paid more – therefore, companies are making more money – therefore, their earnings per share ratios will increase – therefore, current stock values will look cheap – therefore, domestic companies will attract more foreign investment – therefore, their corporate transparency will increase – therefore, their share price will continue to go up – therefore, more companies will float on the domestic stock exchange – therefore, more money will enter into the economy – and so on and so forth.

As one can see from the chart above buying into a nation's changing broad economic architecture – in this case moving from the confines of the Soviet-style system to that of free enterprise and the increased consumerism that this entails – yielded exceptional results for Soros and Rogers.

This example can often be seen in areas that are undergoing such **a shift in behavioural paradigm,** as the same investment curve can be seen across the board, for example, in every country that broke away from the former Soviet Union (Poland, Czech Republic Baltic States etc etc). In this respect, this investment story can be seen as the reverse of negative contagion.

In the case of the former Soviet-Union itself exactly the same theory applied as well, although with a delayed effect to those of its former satellite states, as a break with centralised state control occurred only later on, under the presidency of Boris Yeltsin, which began in December 1991.

For those Top-Down investors who had learned the lesson from what happened to stocks (which are, after all, simply investment in companies, which are in turn an investment on the most basic level in a country's prosperity) in the former satellite nations of the USSR then the opportunity for the next phase of investment was obvious. This could be called a 'moving away from the Communist economic model' play colloquially.

One well-known fund manager, whom I cannot name as he is particularly fond of his and his fund's privacy, saw what had happened in the Former Soviet Union states and anticipated the same occurring in the newly formed Russian Federation after Yeltsin took power, and again the investment profile was identically bullish, as shown in the chart below.

Russian Stock Exchange (RTS) After Yeltsin Took Power

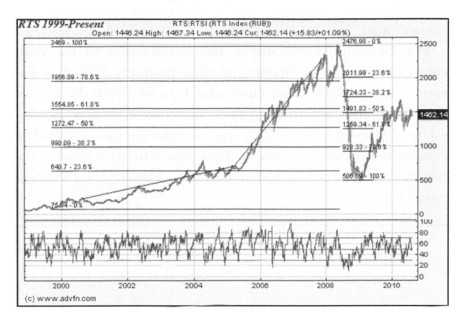

Area-Specific Top-Down Trading (Negative Paradigm Shifts)

At the time that the euro came into play on 1 January 1999, it was obvious to me and many others that have been trading through up and down cycles for many years that it was a fundamentally flawed currency because the eurozone was a fundamentally flawed idea itself.

The reasons for this notion now are exactly the same as they were at the beginning: unlike the USA, which could be regarded as a similar basic concept as the eurozone – that is, a group of separate state economies with one currency (the USD) – the eurozone lacked a true centralised fiscal policy (the use of taxation and expenditure to influence economic prospects).

Principally, it lacked a central tax framework, which meant that taxes in each of the member countries of the eurozone were set at different rates, were collected with a varying degree of efficiency (the southern states of the eurozone were much laxer in collection from the wealthier than the northern states) and money was spent in very different ways.

For Germany, for example, the introduction of the euro meant an effective cheapening of their products abroad as the euro's value against other currencies was less than the former Deutschemark's which meant that exports were cheaper and this led to export-led growth. This can be seen in the chart below showing the country's Balance of Trade (the difference between the monetary value of exports and imports in an economy over a certain period of time).

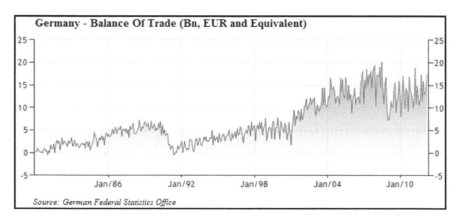

Contrast this to a country for which the introduction of the euro made its products and services more expensive than they were under their previous native currency: Greece (with the drachma formerly) is a notable newsworthy example, but any of the southern eurozone states would show the same pattern, which is either no improvement or a decline over the period from January 1999.

In stock trading terms then this had very clear implications, worsened by the **conceptual difference between those living in the USA and those living in the eurozone**: that is, that although those living for example in New York would view themselves firstly perhaps as New Yorkers they would also see themselves as

Americans, whereas those living in, say, Spain would be unlikely to view themselves as Europeans to such a degree.

Of course, even worse for the dichotomy lying at the very heart of the eurozone is the fact that **although the currencies of the southern states became more expensive relative to their previous currencies, borrowing became a lot cheaper,** as the debt of countries such as Greece, Spain, Italy, Ireland and Portugal, for example, was classed alongside the debt of Germany in terms of its risk profile. This allowed the weaker states to borrow enormous sums at much lower costs than would have been the case before the introduction of the euro, which was spent largely on capital-intensive public sector ventures (and private sector property developments) and led to a huge debt pile.

So, again, the crisis of confidence in Greece then spread, exactly the same way as happened in the former Soviet Union states (but negatively in this case) to the remainder of the countries that were seen as bad credit risks (generally in order of how bad their vulnerability to indebtedness was viewed by the markets).

The markets are a place where traders look for signs of weakness to exploit: 'there's blood in the water' was a common refrain during the sterling currency crisis under Norman Lamont.

So the trick with Top-Down trading is to look beyond the immediate catastrophe for a country – for example Greece or Ireland – and look to sell the indices of the countries that look like they are next in line for the sharks. This is the way you make serious money.

Below, you can clearly see the effect of this contagion on selected markets, from late 2009 when fears about Greece's debt burden started to grow:

Greece Stock Exchange (ASE) Sparks The Hunt For Weak Indices To Sell

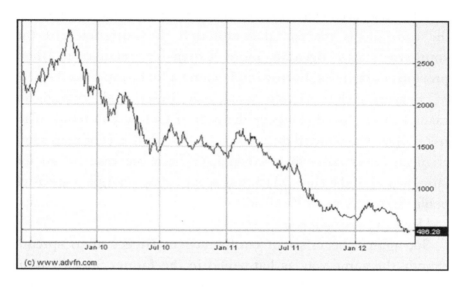

And the following fitted the bill perfectly:

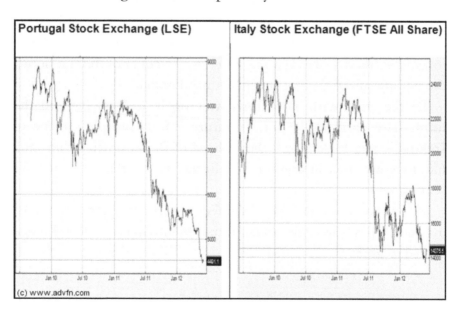

Important Fundamentals
For Top-Down Trading

Interest Rates

Interest rates are perhaps the key determinant in stocks globally (and thus the reason why inflation data is looked at so keenly as, if inflation is rising then interest rates generally are set to rise).

Conversely to currencies, though, domestic equities and indices will tend to go down as local interest rates are raised for four main reasons:

1. The first reason for this is that **as lower-risk investments (bank accounts, savings bonds and so on) increase their return so higher risk investments (equities) will appear less marginally attractive**.

2. The second is that **companies that have borrowed money (for expansion, to cover cashflow requirements or whatever) will have to pay more of their overall capital back in loan repayments and interest thereupon**, which means that they will be less profitable.

3. The third is that that **if the cost of borrowing has gone up for companies then it means that they are less likely to borrow money for corporate expansion**, which again means over time that they will be less likely to grow and thus increase profits.

4. The fourth reason is that **as interest rates rise, the general population are less likely to want to borrow money** (either

through overdrafts or credit cards or whatever) and will broadly spend less, which will hit the revenues of companies.

Effect Of Expectations On Interest Rates (Australia Stock Exchange)

[Chart Key:
A = Australia raises interest rates to 4.5% (back in 2010)
B = Central bank signals that rates will remain steady for the foreseeable future]

Interest rates, in basic terms, are a key tool for a government in managing its economy. **If an economy is becoming overheated (i.e. inflation is increasing to beyond the point at which a government deems it healthy) then interest rates will go up.** This means in practical terms that money becomes more expensive, people spend less, demand decreases, manufacturers cannot increase their prices and thus prices stay the same. And, of course, the converse is true.

The last few years in the West are instructive in this context. In the UK, for example, interest rates were low for many years, meaning that people could borrow money (from banks, on credit cards and so on) for very little in terms of interest repayments. As such, prices increased, the stock market boomed, house prices boomed and people had lots of 'things' (largely things which they did not need, of course). Eventually this resulted in something of a housing and stock market bubble, which has been bursting for the past few years.

(For practical examples see the previous section on Interest Rates And Inflation.)

Credit Ratings

As with people's individual credit ratings that allow them to buy a house or car on credit, a **country's credit rating is a product of market perception about how able it is to generate sufficient income to cover its debts**.

Below shows the deleterious effect on the Greek Stock Exchange of a four notch (grade) downgrade by Moody's on Greece's foreign currency debt profile, to Ba1 from A3.

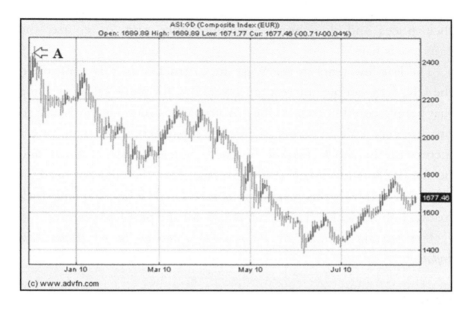

[Chart Key:
A = Point at which Fitch cuts Greece's sovereign credit rating to BBB+ and S&P puts it A- rating on watch for a possible downgrade]

This pattern has been repeated whenever there is speculation that another of the eurozone's fiscally-challenged members may about to be downgraded.

The converse, of course, is true for an upgrade scenario.

(For a full analysis see the previous section on Credit Ratings.)

Here, again, is the chart showing the ratings of the three main credit ratings agencies:

Moody's		S&P		Fitch		
Long-term	Short-term	Long-term	Short-term	Long-term	Short-term	
Aaa		AAA		AAA		Prime
Aa1		AA+	A-1+	AA+	F1+	High grade
Aa2	P-1	AA		AA		
Aa3		AA-		AA-		
A1		A+	A-1	A+	F1	Upper medium grade
A2		A		A		
A3	P-2	A-	A-2	A-	F2	
Baa1		BBB+		BBB+		Lower medium grade
Baa2	P-3	BBB	A-3	BBB	F3	
Baa3		BBB-		BBB-		
Ba1		BB+		BB+		Non-investment grade speculative
Ba2		BB		BB		
Ba3		BB-	B	BB-	B	
B1		B+		B+		Highly speculative
B2		B		B		
B3		B-		B-		
Caa1	Not prime	CCC+				Substantial risks
Caa2		CCC				Extremely speculative
Caa3		CCC-	C	CCC	C	In default with little prospect for recovery
Ca		CC				
		C				
C		D	/	DDD	/	In default
/				DD		

In the current global investment environment, of course, credit ratings are a major pre-occupation for investors of all kinds, not just in equities

As the IMF has been keen to highlight numerous times, the current global financial crisis that began in July 2007 was preceded by the considerable overrating, and hence mispricing, of safety. In this respect, high credit ratings were applied too often, both for private and sovereign issuers, and they did not sufficiently differentiate across assets with different underlying qualities *(see chart below)*.

Historical Overview Of S&P Sovereign Debt Ratings Of Selected OECD Countries (1970-end Jan 2012)

Historical Overview of S&P Sovereign Debt Ratings of Selected OECD Countries, 1970–January 2012											
Country	Year of First Rating	1970	1975	1980	1985	1990	1995	2000	2005	2010	2011	2012 (End-January)
Austria	1975	NR	AAA	AAA	AAA	AAA	AAA	AAA	AAA	AAA	AAA	AA+
Belgium	1988	NR	NR	NR	NR	AA+	AA+	AA+	AA+	AA+	AA	AA
Canada	1949	AAA	AAA	AAA	AAA	AAA	AA+	AA+	AAA	AAA	AAA	AAA
Denmark	1981	NR	NR	NR	AA+	AA	AA+	AA+	AAA	AAA	AAA	AAA
Finland	1972	NR	AAA	AAA	AAA	AAA	AA-	AA+	AAA	AAA	AAA	AAA
France	1975	NR	AAA	AAA	AAA	AAA	AAA	AAA	AAA	AAA	AAA	AA+
Germany	1983	NR	NR	NR	AAA	AAA	AAA	AAA	AAA	AAA	AAA	AAA
Greece	1988	NR	NR	NR	NR	BBB-	BBB-	A-	A	BB+	CC	CC
Iceland	1989	NR	NR	NR	NR	A	A	A+	AA-	BBB-	BBB-	BBB-
Ireland	1988	NR	NR	NR	NR	AA-	AA	AA+	AAA	A	BBB+	BBB+
Italy	1988	NR	NR	NR	NR	AA+	AA	AA	AA-	A+	A	BBB+
Japan	1959	NR[1]	AAA	AAA	AAA	AAA	AAA	AAA	AA-	AA	AA-	AA-
Luxembourg	1994	NR	NR	NR	NR	NR	AAA	AAA	AAA	AAA	AAA	AAA
Netherlands	1988	NR	NR	NR	NR	AAA	AAA	AAA	AAA	AAA	AAA	AAA
Norway	1958	NR[1]	AAA	AAA	AAA	AAA	AAA	AAA	AAA	AAA	AAA	AAA
Portugal	1988	NR	NR	NR	NR	A	AA-	AA	AA-	A-	BBB-	BB
Spain	1988	NR	NR	NR	NR	AA	AA	AA+	AAA	AA	AA-	A
Sweden	1977	NR	NR	AAA	AAA	AAA	AA+	AA+	AAA	AAA	AAA	AAA
Switzerland	1988	NR	NR	NR	NR	AAA	AAA	AAA	AAA	AAA	AAA	AAA
Turkey	1992	NR	NR	NR	NR	NR	B+	B+	BB-	BB	BB	BB
United Kingdom	1978	NR	NR	AAA	AAA	AAA	AAA	AAA	AAA	AAA	AAA	AAA
United States	1941	AAA	AAA	AAA	AAA	AAA	AAA	AAA	AAA	AAA	AA+	AA+

Source: IMF, S&P   AAA AA   A BBB   Noninvestment grade

As it now stands, in the current uncertain environment, **relative asset safety can be seen by considering a continuum of asset characteristics, composed of**: (1) low credit and market risks, (2) high market liquidity, (3) limited inflation risks, (4) low exchange rate risks and (5) limited idiosyncratic risks.

The first criterion, **low credit and market risks, is clearly pivotal to asset safety,** as a lower level of these risks tends to be linked with higher liquidity. However, high market liquidity depends on a wider array of factors, including ease and certainty of valuation, low correlation with risky assets, an active and sizable market and low market correlation, among others.

Importantly, as the IMF has underlined many times, different investors place a different emphasis on each of these criteria. For example, investors with long-term liabilities – such as pension funds and insurance companies – place limited emphasis on market liquidity and thus consider less liquid, longer maturity assets as safe. If their potential payoffs are linked to inflation and no inflation indexed securities are available, pension funds emphasise the real capital preservation aspect of safe assets.

For retail investors in the meantime, the same sort of analysis also holds true, and in this respect the idea that credit ratings agencies are all-knowing should be regarded as a highly dubious proposition to say the least.

This said, of course, there is a vast range of fundamental factors that a stock investor needs to monitor.

Trading The Business Cycle

The business cycle is the recurring level of business activity that changes in patterns in an economy over a period of time. The four stages of a cycle are (although some maintain that there are five): **full scale recession, early recovery, late recovery and early recession.**

Since the Second World War, most business cycles have lasted between three to five years from peak to peak, with the average duration of an expansion being nearly four years and the average length of a recession being just under a year, although as we have seen in the most recent recession (and in the Great Depression era) recessions can last a lot longer.

According to the USA's National Bureau of Economic Research (NBER), the US has experienced 12 recessions (including the current one) and 11 expansions since the end of the Second World War.

US Business Cycles Since 1857 (NBER)

BUSINESS CYCLE REFERENCE DATES		DURATION IN MONTHS			
Peak	Trough	Contraction	Expansion	Cycle	
Quarterly dates are in parentheses		*Peak to Trough*	*Previous trough to this peak*	*Trough from Previous Trough*	*Peak from Previous Peak*
	December 1854 (IV)	--	--	--	--
June 1857(II)	December 1858 (IV)	18	30	48	--
October 1860(III)	June 1861 (III)	8	22	30	40
April 1865(I)	December 1867 (I)	32	46	78	54
June 1869(II)	December 1870 (IV)	18	18	36	50
October 1873(III)	March 1879 (I)	65	34	99	52
March 1882(I)	May 1885 (II)	38	36	74	101
March 1887(II)	April 1888 (I)	13	22	35	60
July 1890(III)	May 1891 (II)	10	27	37	40
January 1893(I)	June 1894 (II)	17	20	37	30
December 1895(IV)	June 1897 (II)	18	18	36	35
June 1899(III)	December 1900 (IV)	18	24	42	42
September 1902(IV)	August 1904 (III)	23	21	44	39
May 1907(II)	June 1908 (II)	13	33	46	56
January 1910(I)	January 1912 (IV)	24	19	43	32
January 1913(I)	December 1914 (IV)	23	12	35	36
August 1918(III)	March 1919 (I)	7	44	51	67
January 1920(I)	July 1921 (III)	18	10	28	17
May 1923(II)	July 1924 (III)	14	22	36	40
October 1926(III)	November 1927 (IV)	13	27	40	41
August 1929(III)	March 1933 (I)	43	21	64	34
May 1937(II)	June 1938 (II)	13	50	63	93
February 1945(I)	October 1945 (IV)	8	80	88	93
November 1948(IV)	October 1949 (IV)	11	37	48	45
July 1953(II)	May 1954 (II)	10	45	55	56
August 1957(III)	April 1958 (II)	8	39	47	49
April 1960(II)	February 1961 (I)	10	24	34	32
December 1969(IV)	November 1970 (IV)	11	106	117	116
November 1973(IV)	March 1975 (I)	16	36	52	47
January 1980(I)	July 1980 (III)	6	58	64	74
July 1981(III)	November 1982 (IV)	16	12	28	18
July 1990(III)	March 1991(I)	8	92	100	108
March 2001(I)	November 2001 (IV)	8	120	128	128
December 2007 (IV)	June 2009 (II)	18	73	91	81
Average, all cycles:					
1854-2009 (33 cycles)		17.5	38.7	56.2	56.4*
1854-1919 (16 cycles)		21.6	26.6	48.2	48.9**
1919-1945 (6 cycles)		18.2	35.0	53.2	53.0
1945-2009 (11 cycles)		11.1	58.4	69.5	68.5

* 32 cycles
** 15 cycles

Source: NBER

Given an identification of which part of the cycle forms the backdrop to your current investment environment, there are some general inferences that you can take regarding which sectors to invest in, as delineated below:

- *Full Scale Recession* (characterised by contracting GDP quarter-on-quarter, falling interest rates, increasing unemployment, declining consumer expectations, among others). Sectors that do well in this environment tend to be: **Cyclicals** (a company's revenues are generally higher in periods of economic prosperity and expansion and lower in periods of economic downturn and contraction, but they can cope easily by reducing wages and workforce during bad times, and include companies that produce durable goods, such as raw materials and heavy equipment), **Transports, Technology and Industrials**.

- *Early Recovery* (consumer expectations are rising, unemployment is falling, industrial production is growing, and interest rates have bottomed out): **Industrials, Basic materials industry and Energy firms**.

- *Late Recovery* (interest rates can be rising rapidly, consumer expectations are beginning to decline, and industrial production is flat): **Energy, Staples and Services**.

- *Early Recession* (Consumer expectations are at their worst; industrial production is falling; interest rates are at their highest): **Services, Utilities, Cyclicals and Transports**.

Bottom-Up Investing

In contrast to Top-Down investing, **this approach attaches much less significance to the broader investment backdrop of economic and market cycles than to a drilled-down-deep analysis of individual stocks.**

The **advantage of this approach is that the investor can spend far less time looking at the multitude of factors that come into play when investing in a Top-Down style**, instead focussing on only one sector first or, in its most pure form, on just one stock irrespective of the sector in which it operates, the country, the geo-political area or anything much else at all for that matter.

Another major advantage is that by taking such a bold focussed approach this type of investor can identify overlooked opportunities that can generate major returns before the attention of Top-Down investors has focussed on the stock by dint of a broad-based market re-assessment of sector, country or area. This means that Bottom-Up investors can catch the first part of a major move on a stock well ahead of the rest of the market in many cases.

Conversely, of course, **the downside is that Bottom-Up investors can be regarded as pioneers in the market, not benefitting from broad-based bull or bear markets** (the trend is not the friend of the Bottom-Up investor) and often has to plough his/her own furrow.

Personally, I believe that using the **best techniques of both strategies is essential to outperformance**.

Having said this, if you are of a particularly bold disposition, there are a number of factors that can help you maximise returns and minimise risk, and we go into these below.

Comparables

Even the most die-hard Bottom-Up trader would be well-advised to look at the comparable performance of companies operating in the same business space as the company that is being investigated for investment.

In general terms, it is **wise to analyse earnings and revenue data, seek to identify trends in both areas and to look at market indicators – such as price/earnings ratio and dividend yield – and compare this data with that for comparable companies in order to see whether a stock offers good value.**

In addition, **looking at a stock's free cash flow** (operating cash flow minus capital expenditures, representing the cash that a company is able to generate after laying out the money required to maintain or expand its asset base) and **forward orders** is also useful, as is looking out for **new products/services** that the company has in the pipeline and at the **company's management history.**

Management

Many of the best **professional global fund managers talk to a company's senior management every six to eight weeks**, and often, as a result of these conversations, their allocation of available assets to a company can fall well short or in excess of a reasonable benchmark.

The ramifications for a company and its stockholders in the choice of its senior management team are virtually always enormous and all the more so in times of broad-based economic adversity such as those currently prevailing.

To begin with, the management needs to be able to **find a balance between having an over-arching vision for the future and possessing an eye for detail, including a very thorough understanding of the company's business and finances.**

In this context, Samir Brikho from AMEC, who took over as CEO in October 2006, is widely regarded as having done a good job of sorting out the company's legacy issues and refocusing the operations for the longer term on the natural resources and power markets.

In this respect, not only did Brikho almost immediately sell off the company's non-core businesses and implement a major cost reduction programme, on a practical note but also focused employees' efforts on achieving a newly clarified company vision ('to be a leading supplier of high value consultancy, engineering and project management services within the world's energy, power and process industries').

A natural, and vitally important, adjunct of being able to **step inside and outside the business is to understand as many of its component elements as possible**. There is a school of thought that takes the view that if you've successfully run one business then you can do the same with any other, whether or not it's in the same business sector or not, but I do not believe that it can be done without taking time out to learn everything you can about the specifics of the firm.

This is true for Sir Terry Leahy, former CEO of Tesco, one of whose principal business tenets was 'keeping a small business mentality within a big business body: the importance of core purpose, values and strategy'. With this approach, Leahy transformed Tesco, over the ten years under his charge, into the number one supermarket in the UK and the third biggest in the world, to a point where it was estimated that one in every eight pounds in the UK was spent in Tesco stores. After he left? Well...

Tesco Share Price After Leahy Announces Retirement

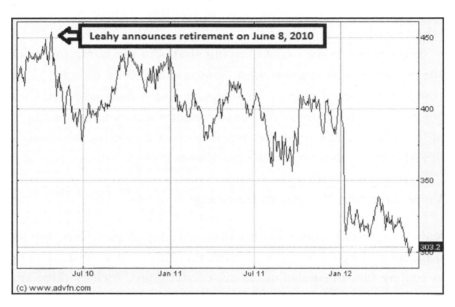

Catching investor attention for a company's senior management team, though, is not always a good thing, particularly given the media glare that surrounds high-profile business figures. Perhaps the most notorious example of this was the overnight destruction of his eponymous British High Street retail chain by the then CEO **Gerald Ratner** who, in 1991, joked (in a speech to the traditionally well-media-covered Institute of Directors get-together) that one of his firm's products was "total crap" and boasted that some of its earrings were "cheaper than a prawn sandwich."

Similarly catastrophic, albeit on a much more rounded basis (gross incompetence plus an arrogant air towards media and shareholders alike) was **George Simpson**'s handling of the then Marconi UK giant in the early 1990s. Interestingly (in a car-crash sort of way), not only did he manage to reduce the company from one with a share price of £12.50 in September 2000 (putting a notional value on the company of £35bn) to one with shares valued at £0.29 (and a notional value of just £807 million) in just one year but he also engineered to pocket a pay-off for himself of over £1 million upon his 'retirement' to a baronial castle in Scotland ('which was nice' as 'The Fast Show' might put it).

Many investors see a **CEO buying shares in the company he or she is head of as a good sign**. This could well be the case – the converse is true, of course, for directors selling their shares in their company. If you want to find out whether a director is investing in his own firm, simply visit the company's home page on the Barclays Stockbrokers website and select the 'Director Deals' tab.

Value Investing Vs Growth Investing

Value investing generally involves buying shares that appear underpriced by some form of fundamental analysis (not the same as trading fundamentals but rather specific ratios, such as discounts to book value, tangible book value, looking at high dividend yield firms, those with low price-to-earnings multiples, low price-to-book ratios, low price-to-cash flow or any combinations thereof). Perhaps the most generally well-known of this type of investor is Warren Buffett and his Berkshire Hathaway fund.

On the other hand, **growth investing involves buying shares in companies that exhibit signs of above-average growth, even if the share price appears expensive in terms of metrics** such as those mentioned directly above.

Key Basic Metrics For Stock Investors

Dividend Yield: as we have seen earlier, generally a higher dividend yield has long been considered to be desirable among many investors (it is after all cash in the hand, quite aside from any other considerations).

Additionally, however, although a high dividend yield can be considered to be evidence that a stock is under-priced, it can also be viewed as evidence that a company's fortunes have deteriorated and that future dividends will not be as high as previous ones.

Similarly a low dividend yield can be considered evidence that the stock is overpriced or that future dividends might be higher.

The formula for calculating this is as follows:

Current dividend yield = most recent full year dividend/current share price.

Book Value: this is the value of an asset according to its account balance as shown on the balance sheet. The value is based on the original cost of the asset less any depreciation, amortisation or impairment costs made against the asset.

Historically, the book value is a company's total assets minus its intangible assets and liabilities. However, in practice and depending on the type of business involved and the type of calculation being employed, book value varies substantially, according to values attributed to goodwill or intangible assets or any combination thereof ('tangible book value' excludes both of the previous two factors).

Earnings Per Share (EPS): this is simply the total amount of earnings for each outstanding share of the company. It does not include preferred dividends for categories outside continued operations and net income.

The formula therefore is:

EPS = profit/weighted average common shares.

Price To Earnings (P/E): this is a measure of the relative price of a share to the annual net income or profit earned by the firm per share:

P/E = market price per share/annual earnings per share.

A lot of emphasis is placed on the P/E ratio by many of investors, as it can be regarded as a prime indicator of the level of confidence that investors have in any given company: clearly, a low P/E would indicate that there is not much to look forward to in terms of growth in earnings, whereas the opposite could be true for a high P/E.

Having said that, there is a danger when P/Es become very high that a bubble is growing about a particular stocks or sector, such as happened in the case of the dot.com bubble (when the average global P/E for such firms was 32).

The average P/E for US equities from 1900 to 2005 was 16 (arithmetic mean), but in many emerging markets where expectations are high and a weight of money is looking for a home (China recently has been a good example of this trend) these P/Es are much higher.

EV/EBITDA: this is the enterprise value (EV, the sum of claims of all the security-holders: debt-holders, preferred shareholders, minority shareholders, common equity holders and others) of a company divided by its earnings before interest, tax, depreciation and amortisation (EBITDA) and is preferred by many to P/E because it is capital structure neutral.

Hedging

A perfect hedge means one in which no risk whatsoever is taken. As a corollary of this, it means that there will also be no reward. The perfect hedge would be, for instance, buying the FTSE100 index and simultaneously selling the same thing. Thus, perfect hedging is a rather pointless exercise.

Instead, hedging as it is actually used is of an imperfect sort which can either: help reduce my overall net losses in a bad position (by making offsetting gains in other related areas) or help add to my overall net profits (whilst not actually proportionately increasing the risk involved). In this sense, then, hedging is a method of dynamically managing the risk/reward profile for the trader.

Let us say that some time ago I had been encouraged – as many were – by positive-sounding mumblings from various eurozone leaders about the efficacy of bailouts and so forth and had gone long a eurozone index, so bought the Greece Stock Exchange (ASE). However, this has proven to be incorrect thus far.

Cross-Equities Hedging

Staying with the fact that I went long of Greece (a eurozone country) I could have hedged this exposure, which is basically an exposure to the fortunes of the euro currency and eurozone member countries as a whole, by **seeking exposure to a non-euro market**, such as the US (and by extension the US dollar).

So, here we have my two positions: long Greece and also a little later long the DJIA.

Let us say that I had believed the reassurances of the eurozone people and gone long Greece at 1165, GBP10 per point (point A in the chart).

Greece Stock Exchange (ASE Composite)

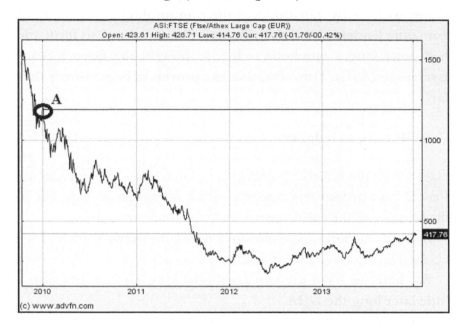

After a while, it became clear that things were not going my way in the short-term, although I still believed that they might improve over the longer-term and was happy to keep the position, so I kept moving my stop-loss (never a good idea, of course). So I look to modify my losses by buying the DJIA as well in the short term, at 10949.00 (Point A in the chart).

US Dow Jones Industrial Average

So, in sum **let's analyse the two positions** to my point of getting out of both – let's say about the middle of March 2012:

Long Greece position = Loss of 1165 to 780 multiplied by GBP10 per point = GBP3,850

Long US position = Gain of 10949 to 13200 multiplied by GBP10 per point = GBP22,510

Overall result of hedging strategy = Profit of GBP18,660.

Alternatively, I could have decided to sell a different eurozone country index, perhaps Portugal, at 6075 (shown as Point A in the chart below).

Portugal Stock Exchange

So, in sum again let's analyse the two positions to my point of getting out of both – let's say about the middle of March 2012 once more:

Long Greece position = Loss of 1165 to 780 multiplied by GBP10 per point = GBP3,850
Short Portugal position = Gain of 8198 to 5100 multiplied by GBP10 per point = GBP30,980.
Overall result of hedging strategy = Profit of GBP27,130.

Cross-Asset Class Hedging

So, **what else could I do to capitalise on the continued poor performance of the eurozone that is crucifying my long Greece index position?**

- *Sell the major stock indices associated with the individual countries performing especially badly in the EUR region* (as shown above).

- Looking at it another way, *I could have bought US stock indices instead/ as well as* (as shown above).

- Or, I could hedge out my risk by *trading in a different asset class altogether* (see below).

- I could have *done an option to hedge risks either side.*

Coming back then to the third point on the above list, how could I have hedged my bad long Greece stock index position in other asset classes? The key here, as with all trading, is to **think laterally**.

What is screwing up my long Greece index position? The lack of faith in the eurozone as a whole. Where is the money being redirected? Anywhere but countries that use the euro? Any other considerations? Yes, because there is also a major geo-political risk involved in trading anything to do with the eurozone (because the whole association may fall apart); money is avoiding risky assets where it can, so hedging through risky assets (such as say Australian dollars) will not work particularly well. Any other considerations? Yes, if the eurozone falls to pieces then its ability to buy goods and services from abroad will diminish markedly which means avoiding any countries that have a major trading connection with the eurozone (the UK for example – around 60% of our exports globally go to eurozone countries).

So, which areas are we left with – that is, where in the world does money go when there is heightened risk (US, Switzerland, gold and PGMs) and what assets are not especially connected to eurozone trade (US dollar, Swiss Franc, gold and PGMs)?

Consequently, if the Greece stock market is falling we could not only hedge by buying US stock markets (as we did above to great effect) or selling other eurozone stock markets (which again we did above to great effect) but also by buying

currencies in those countries that fulfil all of our earlier stated criteria. In this case, we choose the US dollar (USD).

So, here is our basic position again – long Greece stock market at 1165, GBP10 per point.

Greece Stock Exchange (ASE Composite)

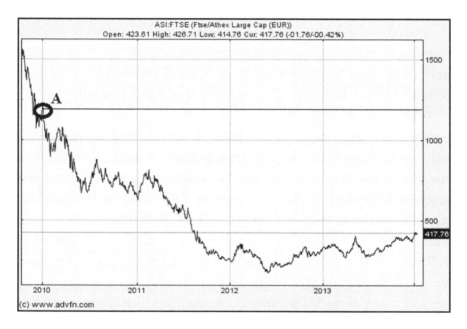

But now we also buy USD. What do we buy it against (i.e. what currency do we sell)? If we are betting against the eurozone then the obvious candidate is to buy USD and sell euros (at 1.3972, as shown in Point A in the chart below).

EURUSD (5 Years, Weekly)

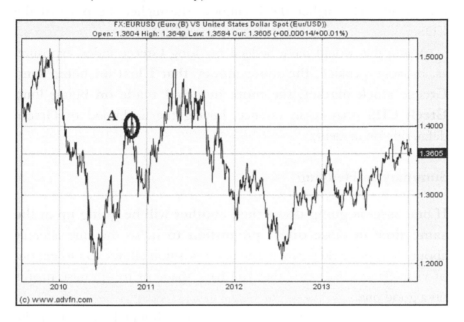

FX:EURUSD (Euro (B) VS United States Dollar Spot (Eur/USD))
Open: 1.3604 High: 1.3649 Low: 1.3584 Cur: 1.3605 (+00.00014/+00.01%)

(c) www.advfn.com

So, the effect of this is:

Long Greece position = Loss of 1165 to 780 multiplied by GBP10 per point = GBP3,850
Sell EUR Buy USD position = Gain of 1.3972 to 1.3070 multiplied by GBP10 per point = GBP9,020.
Overall result of hedging strategy = Profit of GBP5,170.

Cross-Sovereign/Credit Rating Hedging

Given that the credit risk for the troubled eurozone members was increasing over the period when the EUR and eurozone stock indices were falling out of bed, I could buy **credit default swaps** (CDS) on the countries worst affected. **CDS are basically like insurance policies on entities going bankrupt** (for example companies or, in this case, countries) – the more technical definition is: CDS pay the buyer face value in exchange for the underlying securities or the cash equivalent should a government or company fail to adhere to its debt agreements. The higher the likelihood, the higher the price of the CDS.

Again, this would have hedged my long Greece index exposure, as, broadly speaking, **the more money that I lost on being long Greece stock market, the more money I made on being long Greek CDS** (that is, in essence, buying the likelihood of Greece defaulting on its debt).

Summary on Hedging

If one asset is going down then another will be going up at the same time in close direct proportion to it, so thinking laterally about all asset markets when one has a position allows you to get out of virtually any bad trade that you have made or to optimise profits on a good one.

Preferably, as discussed elsewhere, you should know all of the possible trading options available to you across as many asset markets as possible before you enter into the trade in the first place.

And that's about it folks.

Except to say that if you find yourselves getting up in the morning and not feeling excited about the prospect of trading that day then it is probably time to consider something else as a means of earning money.

Good luck.

ABOUT THE AUTHOR

After graduating from Oxford University with BA (Hons) and MA (Hons) degrees, Simon Watkins worked for a number of years as a senior Forex trader and salesman, ultimately achieving the positions of **Director of Forex at Bank of Montreal and Head of Forex Institutional Sales for Credit Lyonnais.** He has since become a **financial journalist, being Head of Weekly Publications And Managing Editor and Chief Writer of Business Monitor International, Head of Global Fuel Oil Products for Platts, Global Managing Editor of Research for Renaissance Capital (Moscow)** and **Head of Developed Market Bond Analysis for Bond Radar.**

He has written extensively on Forex, equities, bonds and commodities for many publications, including: *The Financial Times, Euromoney, FT Capital Insights, FX-MM, CFO Insight, The Edge Middle East Finance, International Commerce Magazine, The Securities And Investment Review, Accountancy Magazine, The Emerging Markets Monitor, Asia Economic Alert, Latin America Economic Alert, Eastern Europe*

Economic Alert, Oil And Gas Middle East, European CEO, Global Finance Magazine, World Finance Magazine, The Emerging Markets Report, FTSE Global Markets, VM Group Energy Monthly, VM Group Metals Monthly, Islamic Investor Magazine, Finance Europe, Finance Emerging Europe and *CIMA Financial Management.*

In addition, he has worked as an investment consultant for major hedge funds in London, Moscow and the Middle East.

MORE BOOKS FROM ADVFN

101 CHARTS FOR
TRADING SUCCESS

by Zak Mir

Using insider knowledge to reveal the tricks of the trade, Zak Mir's *101 Charts for Trading Success* explains the most complex set ups in the stock market.

Providing a clear way of predicting price action, charting is a way of making money by delivering high probability percentage trades, whilst removing the need to trawl through company accounts and financial ratios.

Illustrated with easy to understand charts this is the accessible, essential guide on how to read, understand and use charts, to buy and sell stocks. *101 Charts* is a must for all future investment millionaires.

THE GAME
IN WALL STREET

by Hoyle and Clem Chambers

As the new century dawned, Wall Street was a game and the stock market was fixed. Ordinary investors were fleeced by big institutions that manipulated the markets to their own advantage and they had no comeback.

The Game in Wall Street shows the ways that the titans of rampant capitalism operated to make money from any source they could control. Their accumulated funds gave the titans enormous power over the market and allowed them to ensure they won the game.

Traders joining the game without knowing the rules are on a road to ruin. It's like gambling without knowing the rules and with no idea of the odds.

The Game in Wall Street sets out in detail exactly how this market manipulation works and shows how to ride the price movements and make a profit.

And guess what? The rules of the game haven't changed since the book was first published in 1898. You can apply the same strategies in your own investing and avoid losing your shirt by gambling against the professionals.

Illustrated with the very first stock charts ever published, the book contains a new preface and a conclusion by stock market guru Clem Chambers which put the text in the context of how Wall Street operates today.

THE DEATH OF WEALTH

by Clem Chambers

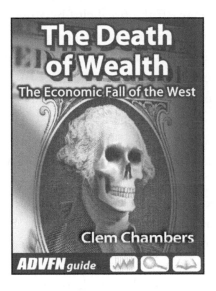

Question: what is the next economic game changer?
Answer: The Death of Wealth.

Market guru Clem Chambers dissects the global economy and the state of the financial markets and lays out the evidence for the death of wealth.

The Death of Wealth flags up the milestones on the route towards impending financial disaster. From the first tentative signs of recovery in the UK and US stock markets at the start of 2012, to the temporary drawing back from the edge of the Fiscal Cliff at the end, the book chronicles the trials and tribulations of the markets throughout the year.

Collecting together articles and essays throughout the last twelve months along with extensive new analysis for 2013, *The Death of*

Wealth allows us to look at these tumultuous events collectively and draw a strong conclusion about what the future holds.

2012 started with the US economy showing signs of recovery, and European financial markets recovering some of the ground lost during the euro crisis. It ended with Obama's re-election and the deal that delayed the plunge off the fiscal cliff by a few months.

In between, the eurozone crisis continued, but none of the affected countries actually left the eurozone; quantitative easing tried to turn things around with the consequences of these "unorthodox" actions yet unknown; and the equity markets after the mid-year correction became strongly bullish.

The Death of Wealth takes you through the events of 2012 month by month, with charts showing the movements of the FTSE 100, the NASDAQ COMPX and the SSE COMPX throughout the year.

With an introduction by renowned market commentator and stock tipster Tom Winnifrith and a summary by trading technical analyst Zak Mir, this collection chronicles the rocky road trip the financial systems of the world have been on and predicts the ultimate destination: the death of wealth as we know it.